THE NATIONAL ASSOCIATION OF REALTORS®

THE NATIONAL ASSOCIATION OF REALTORS®

GUIDE TO

Home Buying

 NATIONAL ASSOCIATION OF REALTORS®

The Voice for Real Estate®

with Blanche Evans

John Wiley & Sons, Inc.

Copyright © 2007 by NATIONAL ASSOCIATION OF REALTORS®. All rights reserved.

Published by John Wiley & Sons, Inc., Hoboken, New Jersey.
Published simultaneously in Canada.

For general information on our other products and services or for technical support, please contact our Customer Care Department within the United States at (800) 762-2974, outside the United States at (317) 572-3993 or fax (317) 572-4002.

Wiley also publishes its books in a variety of electronic formats. Some content that appears in print may not be available in electronic books. For more information about Wiley products, visit our web site at www.wiley.com.

Library of Congress Cataloging-in-Publication Data:

National Association of Realtors.
    The National Association of Realtors® guide to home buying / The
National Association of Realtors® with Blanche Evans.
      p.   cm.
    ISBN-13: 978-0-470-03789-8 (pbk.)
    ISBN-10: 0-470-03789-X (pbk.)
    1. House buying. 2. Home ownership. I. Evans, Blanche. II. Title.
III. Title: Guide to home buying.
    HD1379.N358   2006
    643'.12—dc22

                                            2006013569

Printed in the United States of America.

10 9 8 7 6 5 4 3 2 1

Contents

Acknowledgments

The NATIONAL ASSOCIATION OF REALTORS® thanks Blanche Evans for her time, expertise, and dedication to this project.

NAR would like to thank the following people for their valuable contributions in the creation of this publication: Bob Goldberg, Laurie Janik, David Lereah, Frank Sibley, Pat Kaplan, Pamela Williams, Matt Lombardi, Ken Burlington, Mary Martinez, Thomas Doyle, Paul Bishop, Dan Schmitz, and Larry Jellen. NAR also thanks the following groups for their support: the Real Estate Buyer's Agent Council (REBAC); the staff at *REALTOR® Magazine Online*; and Jody Lane and the staff at *Realty Times*.

In addition, special thanks go to our editor, Laurie Harting, and the team at John Wiley & Sons for all of their support for this project.

Blanche Evans would like to thank the wonderful staff at the NATIONAL ASSOCIATION OF REALTORS®, specifically Ken

Burlington, Pamela Williams, Bob Goldberg, Frank Sibley, Stacey Moncrieff, and Steve Cook, with special kudos to chief economist David Lereah and his fine research staff.

Special thanks also goes to Jody Lane, founder of *Realty Times*, *Realty Times TV*, and RealtyTimes.com. Without his support and encouragement, and occasional borrowing of the services of our terrific copy editor, Carla Davis, this project would not have been possible.

Laurie Harting of John Wiley & Sons has been a delight, and her guidance and ability to keep everyone on schedule and on track are appreciated.

It is an honor beyond imagining to be able to provide the voice for "The Voice for Real Estate®"—the NATIONAL ASSOCIATION OF REALTORS®.

Introduction

Whether you are a first-time, lifestyle-adjusting, or investment-minded home buyer, there's information you need to know and there are steps you need to take to get the best possible home at the most affordable price and terms.

The NATIONAL ASSOCIATION OF REALTORS® Guide to Home Buying is a user-friendly, comprehensive, and concise book to help you achieve your dream of home ownership using the professional knowledge and experience of the largest homeowner lobbying group and trade organization in the world—the NATIONAL ASSOCIATION OF REALTORS® (NAR).

NAR has partnered with respected real estate journalist Blanche Evans, editor of *Realty Times* (www.realtytimes.com), the Internet's largest real estate news and advice source, to bring you the most objective and resourceful guide to home buying possible.

Who better to assist you through the confusing maze of choices you'll be making in finding the right agent, loan and lender, type of home, neighborhood, Internet home buying sources, and much more?

This comprehensive guide provides you with important questions you need to ask yourself and options you need to consider to guide you through the home buying process, including:

- Hiring the right real estate agent.
- The true costs and rewards of home ownership.
- Deciding how much home to buy.
- Preparing your finances to buy.
- Finding the right lender and loan program to meet your needs.
- Shopping for homes.
- Choosing the right community and lifestyle.
- The advantages and disadvantages of new homes versus existing, or resale, homes.
- Making your offer.
- Steps of the typical transaction.
- The final walk-through.
- Who pays for what?
- Moving day tips.

Use the tips and tricks in this book to help you learn about real estate and lending web sites, for-sale-by-owner sellers, types of properties to consider, and how to buy the most home for the best terms and price.

What You Will Learn from This Book

In all things, timing is everything. You will learn whether it is the right time to buy a home and what you can do to improve your position to buy the best home for the money.

You'll learn how to choose the right real estate agent and what kind of representation is open to you as the buyer.

You'll learn how to prepare your finances so you can figure how much home you can truly afford and which kind of loan poses the least risk and greatest benefit to you.

You'll learn the best ways to shop for a home, the importance of choosing the right neighborhood, and which features are important to have. You'll compare the advantages of new construction versus existing homes and learn how to work with builders. You'll learn when homes are functionally obsolete and what upgrades are appropriate.

You'll learn about housing markets and the strategies for making the best deal possible. You'll learn the ins and outs of contracts, inspections, and appraisals, and what you'll need to know to close the deal.

Finally, moving day will come. You'll finish with easy tips for moving and settling into your new home.

So, sit back, get out your highlighter, and let the real estate experts help you get started using the latest and most effective home buying techniques!

About the NATIONAL ASSOCIATION OF REALTORS®

The NATIONAL ASSOCIATION OF REALTORS® (NAR), "The Voice for Real Estate®," is the largest trade organization in the United States, with more than 1.2 million members. Membership is composed of residential and commercial members who are brokers, salespeople, property managers, appraisers, counselors, and other related professionals.

The term REALTOR® is a registered membership mark. Only NAR members are allowed to call themselves REALTORS®, and to wear and display the easily recognizable blue REALTOR® R. As members, they've committed to abide by NAR's strict Code of Ethics and Standards of Practice.

What does that mean to you? While its mission is to help members become more profitable and successful, NAR is also intent on raising the standard of professional practice, ethics, and behavior for its members to follow. Consumers should know the difference and ask their agents if they are "REALTORS®."

Since 1908, NAR has influenced the buying and selling of real estate in profound ways by providing facilities for professional development, research, and communication between the industry and the public and government. Without NAR, the free enterprise system with regard to the right to own, use, and transfer real property might be more expensive and offer far fewer benefits to owners than it does now.

Composed primarily of state-licensed real estate agents and brokers, NAR has three organizational levels—local, state, and national. Members belong to more than 1,400 local associations/boards in 54 states and territories.

REALTORS® use their membership clout to lobby for homeowner and industry issues at all levels. Many of the homeowner benefits that exist today are a direct result of lobbying efforts by NAR, including:

- Federal tax relief and homeowner incentives (Tax Relief Act of 1997).
- Mortgage interest rate deductions.
- Lower real estate taxes.
- Local tax benefits.
- Low-income assistance programs.
- Higher ceilings on federally insured loans for expensive markets.
- Tax-free gains on primary residences, owner-occupied two out of five years—$500,000 for married couples, $250,000 for singles.

- Protections from mortgage fraud and predatory lending.
- Freedom of choice in real estate agent selection and type of representation.

The list goes on and on. So remember, when you hire a REALTOR®, you're really putting the strength of more than 1.2 million members in your corner.

Why Use a REALTOR®?

Over 85 percent of consumers use a real estate agent to buy or sell their homes. That's because buying or selling a home is one of the biggest financial challenges any consumer is likely to ever face. While the rewards are great, there are a number of financial and legal risks attached to buying property. A REALTOR® can help you sidestep pitfalls that could otherwise spoil your enjoyment of your home.

For buyers, your agent is equipped to help you obtain financing so you'll be able to shop for homes with confidence that you are buying in your range. Your agent will help you find the right home using a wide variety of tools, from his/her association membership and access to the local multiple listing service (MLS), to for-sale-by-owner properties, to networking with fellow agents, clients, and contacts to find properties that aren't yet on the market. She or he will help you negotiate terms that are favorable for your finances, your moving date, and your goals.

Depending on the relationship you develop with your agent, you might find that some go much further, helping you to clean up your credit, working with you to help establish yourself as a home buyer and/or investor, finding you service technicians, and much more that isn't part of an agent's usual services.

In choosing a REALTOR®, you will have an agent who is committed to NAR's strict Code of Ethics, which is based on professionalism and protection of the public. That's why all real estate licensees are not the same. Ongoing ethics training is a mandatory requirement of NAR and a good way for you to know that your agent is accountable for his or her actions through disciplinary sanctions beyond those provided at the state and/or local level.

NAR members are required to be honest with and ethical to all parties involved in the transaction—buyer, seller, and cooperating agent. REALTORS® build their business on their reputations. The greatest honor you can do your REALTOR® is to recommend him/her to your friends and family.

About Blanche Evans and *Realty Times*

Since 1997, Blanche Evans and *Realty Times* (www.realtytimes.com) have been the Internet source for consumer and industry real estate news and advice. Independently owned and operated, *Realty Times* is not only a leading content provider, but also the sponsor of *Realty Times TV*, which provides home buying and selling news and advice to consumers while showcasing REALTOR® listings from around the country.

Blanche Evans is the editor of *Realty Times* and a contributor to *Realty Times TV*. She has been recognized by the editors of *REALTOR® Magazine* as one of the 25 Most Influential People in Real Estate, and one of the few women recognized at the Notable level or above more than once. She is the author of numerous books, magazine articles, and white papers about the real estate industry, and is a well-received speaker at industry events. She is frequently interviewed by the media about consumer real estate issues and is widely regarded as one of the most knowledgeable people in the industry.

Realty Times is not associated with NAR, but over the years, the two organizations have found they have objectives in common—the desire to serve consumers while promoting higher industry standards for real estate professionals.

CHAPTER 1

When Is It Time to Consider Owning Your Own Home?

Food, clothing, shelter. Those are the most basic of human needs. In the new millennium, we've taken these foundations for living from the primitive to the most sophisticated. Today, we're gourmets, fashionistas, and housing experts. Just as we express preferences in what we eat and what we wear, we are finding that housing is far more than shelter. It's a means of expression—a lifestyle.

Finding shelter appeals to the migratory creature in all of us. When you leave your family's nest to establish a home of your own, you're tapping into a primordial urge to establish new frontiers. The trick is not to merely survive, but to thrive—and to make your choices wisely, not only so that you are the most comfortable and happy that you can be, but so you can profit when you are ready to move on.

That means you have a choice about where and how you want to live. The question is, what do you really want, and what's within your means? There's a lot to consider, from timing to finances to selecting the right property to buy.

To Rent or to Buy

If you are like 40 percent of home buyers, your annual income is about $57,200 and you are buying a home for the first time. Thanks to your credit files and scores (see Chapter 3), which help determine your loan rate and the amount you wish to borrow, you may qualify to buy a home priced as high as $200,000, at 6.25 percent on a 30-year note, according to mortgage expert and author David Reed. Your monthly payments would work out to about $1,650, or 34 percent of your annual income. That opens up a wide range of properties for you to consider in lots of locations, prices, types, and sizes of homes.

The first decision you have to make is whether to rent or to buy, and there are plenty of arguments for both sides.

The Case for Renting

Renting is no longer merely the default choice of those who are just starting new jobs post-graduation, or who don't have the credit scores or have not saved a down payment to buy a home.

Many people choose to rent because of the relative lack of responsibility and the increased freedom that comes from not owning. Because the landlord can often maintain the property through management services, renters are generally free of maintenance duties, although there are reasonable expectations of care.

Some feel that renting offers more than buying, such as shared access to otherwise unaffordable amenities like swimming pools, spas, fitness centers, conference facilities, club rooms, and planned community events. If you want to meet people, it's hard to find a place more fun than an active apartment community.

Renting is a short-term commitment. Compared to the years of equity building required when owning a home before it can be sold at a profit, rental and lease terms are comparatively easy to get in and out of. You simply have to meet the deposit terms, make your rent payment on time, and keep your place in the same shape it was when the keys were turned over to you. While you rent, you can spend that six months or a year making plans for your next move, even if you decide to stay put.

The longer you stay under the same rental agreement with the landlord, the longer your costs are fixed. You sign a contract that says no matter what happens in the world—high oil prices or a housing boom—your rent payment will stay the same for the term of the lease. That can be reassuring for someone who is trying to pay off a student loan or who wants to save to buy a home.

Renting is financially appealing in other ways. With one or two month's rent as a deposit, and a few hundred thrown in to cover potential carpet replacement because of your pet dog or cat, you can sign for the right to occupy someone else's space. Renting gives you time to prioritize and put your money toward other goals, like buying a home, starting a business, or getting married and having children. For older renters, it's a chance to regroup and prioritize finances as they undergo life changes such as divorce, the death of a spouse, a new job, or a move to a new city.

Homeowners, unlike renters, can make money buying and selling their home, but to do so, they must cover the costs of the purchase and sale transactions. When you think of the costs to buy a home and sell it, including lender fees, attorneys' fees, sales commissions, title searches and policies, inspections, appraisal fees, and other fees, it's easy to see why people don't frequently move in and out of homes they buy. In fact, homeowners are likely to stay in their homes for four to seven years before moving again.

That's why renting is best when you know you won't be staying for long (about two years or less) or when you have other priorities than the responsibilities of home ownership. But being carefree has its price. When you rent, you are paying for predictability—that prices won't go up for the term of your lease, broken appliances will be fixed, and you will have more free time. The downside is you aren't building equity for yourself, but for someone else. To come out ahead as a renter, you must be disciplined about saving—socking away the difference you would be spending if you were the owner.

To have a good experience as a renter, you have to be a good renter. It's all about relationships. The owner wants the property kept in good working order with no complaints to tend to about wild parties, dangerous pets, unauthorized tenants, and so on. If you've been a good renter, your good relationship with the owner may help you cruise through potential problems. If you're suddenly transferred by your company, for example, your landlord may keep your security deposit but allow you to exit your lease without further penalty.

But if you prefer to do whatever you want (within reason), like paint your walls green and purple, or build wealth for yourself instead of for someone else, maybe it's time to think about the benefits of home ownership.

Owning a Home—the American Dream

The number one reason for buying a home is the desire to own, an attitude proudly shared by both first-time and repeat home buyers. This is particularly true of first-time home buyers who see home ownership as the way to accumulate equity, take advantage of generous government tax benefits, and enjoy surveying and customizing their domicile to their personal liking.

Other reasons for owning a home include the desire for more space—space you can change according to your needs and preferences. For example, you may be adding to your family and want a home with a playroom, study area, and backyard so the family can enjoy a variety of activities beyond what your one-bedroom, one-living-area rental may allow.

Or you may want less space as you grow older and your children leave the nest. That's the time to enjoy more luxurious appointments, with less square footage and yard to worry about.

Seven Reasons to Own Your Own Home

1. *Tax breaks.* The U.S. Tax Code lets you deduct the interest you pay on your mortgage, property taxes you pay, and some of the costs involved in buying your home.

2. *Gains.* Since 1989, national home prices increased at an average of 5.5 percent annually. And while there's no guarantee of appreciation, it is estimated that, through price gains and reducing mortgages through payment of principle, a typical homeowner has $144,000 in equity in a home, based on data from the Federal Reserve.[1]

3. *Equity.* Money paid for rent is money that you'll never see again, but mortgage payments let you build equity ownership interest in your home.

4. *Savings.* Building equity in your home is a ready-made savings plan. And when you sell, you can generally take up to $250,000 ($500,000 for a married couple) as gain without owing any federal income tax.

5. *Predictability.* Unlike rent, fixed mortgage payments don't go up over the years, so your housing costs may actually decline as you own the home longer. (*Note:* Adjustable mortgages may change if there is a change in interest rates.) However, keep in mind that property taxes and insurance costs may rise.

6. *Freedom.* The home is yours. You can decorate any way you want and be able to benefit from your investment for as long as you own the home.

7. *Stability.* Remaining in one neighborhood for several years gives you a chance to participate in community activities, lets you and your family establish lasting friendships, and offers your children the benefit of educational continuity.

[1]"Flow of Funds Accounts of the United States," Federal Reserve Statistical Release, Table B.100 (www.federalreserve.gov/releases/z1/current/default.htm).

(Copyright 2006. Reprinted with permission from REALTOR® Magazine Online.)

Perhaps an exciting job opportunity is taking you to a new destination where you'll be living for a while. Perhaps your company has a history of transferring executives like yourself for two or three years per area. In most cases, that's long enough to buy a home, enjoy it for the duration, and sell at a profit.

No matter what your reason, owning a home affords you a number of tax and investment benefits that aren't available to renters. Take advantage of this if owning makes sense for you financially and emotionally. If you've decided you're ready, here's what you'll have to look forward to.

Your Home as an Investment

Your home is a major investment and, as for most Americans, it is your largest financial asset and a major player in your investment portfolio, especially if you are diversified into stocks, bonds, and other instruments. Maybe you aren't quite there yet, and are still paying off student loans, credit card debt, and other responsibilities before thinking of investments. If so, owning a home is a good way to build wealth.

The NATIONAL ASSOCIATION OF REALTORS® estimates that home values have risen since 1989, on average, by 5.5 percent which is well ahead of the annual inflation rate of approximately 3.5 percent. While some markets have been known to report tremendous gains or losses due to extraordinary events, there has never been a year that housing has lost value nationwide—not since NAR began keeping records back in the 1960s.

According to those suggested averages, assuming you are buying a starter home at $110,000, your home will be worth $114,950 after one year of ownership (because its value will have increased 4.5 percent) and it will be worth $120,123 after two years at 4.5 percent annual appreciation. In 10 years, it will be worth $163,470, and so on.

With home ownership, you not only earn a return on your original purchase price, but you get a return on your appreciation. There's not another investment that works quite like that with so little risk.

You Can't Afford Not to Buy a Home

Home ownership is the traditional starting point for American families to accumulate wealth, according to studies by NAR.

Since record keeping began in 1968, the national median home price has risen every year, even during recessions and periods of sales decline. Typically, home values rise at the general rate of inflation, plus one to two percentage points.

To date, inflation has typically averaged about 3.5 percent annually, as mentioned previously, with home price gains a percentage point or more above that. During some periods, inflation is much higher, as much as 5 or 6 percent, eating into home gains, while recently, many areas of the nation have experienced a housing boom where home values have skyrocketed well beyond inflation. Some coastal areas as well as many inland cities have reported home price gains in the double digits.

Since 2000, housing prices have virtually doubled nationwide, and some areas have doubled annually, due to a series of economic factors that are unprecedented.

- The Tax Relief Act of 1997 and other local and national tax benefits assure homeowners that they will be able to sell their homes and keep their profits without paying capital gains tax in most cases. If you are a homeowner who has occupied your property for two out of five years, you can sell your home and keep the capital gains up to $250,000 if you are unmarried, and $500,000 as a married couple.

- Property taxes and mortgage interest are currently deductible from income taxes. In some municipalities, city leaders are working to lower property taxes for homeowners.

- Historically low interest rates and easy, low down payment or interest-only loans have encouraged people to put their money into housing because of the relatively low risk and high return on someone else's money.

- The stock market plunge of 2000 and the subsequent ethics scandals of many corporate leaders have led many investors to turn away from the stock market in favor of housing, over which they may feel they have more control. In 2005, more than a quarter of housing purchases were by non-occupying owners, suggesting that housing has become the investment of choice for many.

- Rising immigration, the wealth of baby boomers, and the coming of age of echo boomers (people born between 1982 and 1995) as home buyers means that the market for housing is only going to improve with the growing population.

■ Dollar for dollar, the rate of return on an individual's cash down payment on a house is substantial. Home buyers typically use their own money to cover only a small portion of the purchase price, yet the home appreciation they realize is based on the total value of the property. (First-time home buyers make a median down payment of 2 percent, while repeat buyers put 21 percent down—thanks to the equity they built in their previous home.)

While there are many reasons to buy a home, the point is that cumulatively speaking, there is no better time to do so. Even if a few of these favorable conditions change, home ownership is a cherished institution in the United States, and is heavily subsidized by the government at both the national and local levels.

One way the government encourages home ownership is by helping banks increase the supply of money that they have to lend to home buyers, through the establishment of a secondary market that buys mortgages and packages them into securities. The government also establishes criteria for *conforming* and *non-conforming* loans, which allows borrowers to qualify for the best mortgage interest rates possible.

Buying a home should be approached as a long-term investment, providing both equity accumulation and tax benefits over time. In addition, over the last few years, some home buyers have shown a readiness to pull their money out of stocks and put it into real estate, often for a second home—a wise and practical move that provides safe returns in a tangible asset. In fact,

36 percent of home sales in 2004 were second homes, including 23 percent for investment purposes. By 2006, 28 percent of homes were sold to investors.

According to "State of the Nation's Housing Report 2005" by Harvard University's Joint Center for Housing Studies, there is a dramatic increase in the rate of return on housing the longer it is held. For instance, the typical homeowner who experiences an annual home appreciation rate of 5 percent and who made a cash down payment of 10 percent will generally receive a 94 percent return on that cash after owning the home only three years. After owning for five years, a homeowner can expect the rate of return on the down payment to increase to 225 percent; after 10 years, the rate of return jumps to 623 percent.

Housing is not a quick-in, quick-out investment. When purchased for the long term, housing is one of the safest investments a consumer can make. In addition to the savings accumulated through a buildup of equity and tax advantages, a home provides shelter. No paper investment provides this benefit.

Homeowners may use their home equity to get cash for emergencies as well as for the purchase of big-ticket items, and have more confidence in housing wealth gains than stock gains that could prove to be unsustainable. In addition, the capital gains people realize from the sale of their home are a significant source of down payment funds for most repeat buyers; those funds are also used for other purposes that stimulate the economy through consumer spending.

In short, homeowners accumulate significantly more wealth than renters. Clearly, owning a home is the best way for most families to build a nest egg.

If you are looking to build wealth; improve your quality of living by choosing a home that best suits the needs of yourself, your partner, and/or your family; and enjoy the benefits of becoming part of a community, it's time for you to buy a home.

CHAPTER 2

Working with Professionals

Choosing the right real estate agent is as important as choosing an attorney, a financial planner, or any other trusted adviser/consultant. For the goal of buying or selling a home, your agent is like a partner who wants the same things you do: for you to find the right home at the right price and for the transaction to go as smoothly as possible.

Along with your mortgage lender, home inspector, insurance agent, title insurer, attorney, and others, your real estate agent is part of your home buying team. Your agent can help you find homes, recommend a list of lenders, point out pitfalls with certain housing types, and ask the right questions of sellers, builders, and others involved with the home. Generally speaking, their job is to get you past the many obstacles that may come up between the time you decide to buy a home and when you close your deal.

The Difference between a REALTOR® and an Agent

All real estate agents are licensed by their states, but only REALTORS® are members of the NATIONAL ASSOCIATION OF REALTORS®. These professionals agree to abide by a higher standard of practice known as the REALTOR® Code of Ethics. In addition, they undergo continuing education and many pursue certifications and designations that distinguish their practices and enhance their experience.

According to the consumer section of NAR's web site (www.REALTOR.org/home_buyers_and_sellers/index.html), "Agents who represent buyers or sellers owe their clients a duty to place their client's interests first. In many states, agents are required by law to provide consumers with information setting forth their terms before embarking on a transaction."

Here are seven reasons to hire a real estate licensee, regardless of whether that person is a REALTOR®, to help you find a home and negotiate your transaction to a successful closing.

1. *Real estate professionals are market specialists.* No matter where you want to live, your housing market favors either sellers or buyers. Your agent will help you prepare to buy a home, from helping you get prequalified for a loan with a

lender, to educating you about the current market conditions, to helping you with your selection.

2. *Real estate professionals are neighborhood experts.* While they are licensed to help you anywhere in the state, most real estate professionals wisely limit themselves to certain neighborhoods or types of homes such as new homes or condominiums. If you've never owned a new home before, your agent can help you understand the building process, ask the right questions of the builder, and negotiate with the builder. For example, in some market areas, builders are asking buyers to pay for title policies, which is not standard when buying a pre-owned home.

3. *Real estate professionals have more information about homes than you do.* While it's fun to drive through neighborhoods and pop into open houses, you may not realize there are homes for sale that you'll never see unless you are working with an agent. Some homes are sold without ever going into the local multiple listing service (MLS). Also, while you can get *comparables*—side-by-side comparative analyses of useful statistics on homes for sale as well as homes that have recently sold—from Internet sites, many of which use automated home valuations as a means to lead you to real estate agents, these online calculations aren't always accurate. (These are also known as a *comparable market analysis,* or CMAs.) Your agent may know why one comparable home sold for more or less than another because she's been inside the houses. Real estate professionals know which houses were updated, which weren't, which have floor plan problems, and so on. This is hands-

on information that can't be learned using an automated online home valuation tool.

4. *Real estate professionals save you time.* If you want to find a home quickly, put an agent to work for you. Over four-fifths of homes for sale in the United States are represented by agents, but an agent acting as your buyer's representative can also help you find homes by builders and for-sale-by-owner sellers and help you negotiate with these nonlisted sellers.

5. *Real estate professionals can work with you the way you want to work.* If you were in court, you'd want a good attorney by your side. As a real estate buyer, you also want an advocate. You can hire an agent as your exclusive fiduciary, which means he or she can't represent the seller at the same time. Or you can hire a transactional broker who can handle both sides of the transaction without fiduciary preference to either side. While these agents are frequently paid on the back end of the transaction at closing, you can also hire an agent to perform certain tasks for an up-front fee such as creating a comparable analysis for you or negotiating the contract on a home for you that you have already found for yourself.

6. *Real estate professionals share your risk.* With an agent by your side, you'll be less likely to make uninformed decisions because you'll know what issues you should consider carefully and why. All houses are imperfect, but some are more imperfect than others. While real estate agents don't take the place of home inspectors or contractors, they can certainly tell you what it will take to bring the home up to the market's standards.

7. *Real estate professionals know how to close a deal.* Finding a home is the easy part. Getting the transaction to closing is the challenge, as so many factors can derail a home purchase. Buyers like you must be helped to overcome obstacles as diverse as inaccurate credit report problems that may take weeks to remove, or rising interest rates that knock you out of qualifying range. And just when everything seems under control, the title company finds out about an undisclosed seller (like an ex-spouse) who doesn't want to sell. Homeowner's insurance companies that withdraw from certain markets due to mold or damage from natural disasters cut new buyers off without warning (as recently happened in California and Texas). Seller disclosures or inspection reports may reveal big problems with your purchase. Your loan may not close on time because you waited too long to lock in your rate. Your seller may attempt to accept another offer that's higher than yours. An agent will know exactly whom to call and what to do to solve any issue that threatens to knock you out of your new home.

Buyers and sellers share the same ultimate goal but have different priorities for achieving it. You want your new house for the least amount of money and the best terms possible. The seller wants the most money and the best terms, too. It takes a skilled negotiator to keep the transaction moving forward.

Yes, you can buy a home on your own, but the rewards of working with an agent can be so much greater. Why would you want to go it alone when you can get exposed to more homes that are right for you and your family's needs, save time finding your home, and lower the risk of losing your transaction to something preventable or salvageable? Hire a real estate agent, and save your energy for moving day.

Licensing Categories, Designations, and Certifications

In most states, with Colorado as a notable exception, there are two types of real estate licensees:

1. *Broker.* A broker has the highest level of real estate licensing. She can operate a brokerage and supervise salespeople who are also licensed by the state. Brokers can be managing brokers, which means the broker in charge, or they can serve as associate brokers with no company management duties. Salespeople report to the managing broker and do business according to the broker's business model. When you sign a representation agreement, you are contracting with the managing broker, even though you may be working with the broker's agent—a salesperson or associate broker.

2. *Salesperson.* A real estate salesperson is licensed to sell and manage real estate but acts as an *agent* of the broker. Your representation contract is actually with the broker, with your salesperson acting as the broker's agent.

Real estate agents also come in various stages of experience, from newly licensed to seasoned veterans. To maintain their licenses, most real estate professionals are required to take continuing education courses to keep up with the changes in the law, state regulations, and local market rules.

Just as other professionals pursue higher education to hone their skills, real estate agents can do the same by becoming members and meeting the educational and business practice requirements of higher-level real estate organizations, particularly associations and nonprofit organizations that serve the real estate industry.

The real estate industry has been quick to meet the needs of buyers and sellers through professional development of its licensees. What these specially earned designations and certifications mean to you is that your agent has achieved customer service mastery in a given niche—the Internet, serving seniors, relocation, buyer's representation, and much more. That's not to say that certification-bearing agents can only help you in that particular niche, but it does mean they have higher education and experience in that area.

Agents who go to the extra effort of putting in the time and expense to acquire designations and certifications not only are showing special interest in their business but are demonstrating a desire to achieve a higher expertise in their profession. That is not to say that you wouldn't be as well served by someone who is new to the field or by a veteran who doesn't have extra credentials, but the chances are greater that a higher degree of professionalism will be demonstrated by someone who has gone the extra mile.

Members of NAR affiliate organizations and other real estate industry trade organizations are able to bring to each other networking skills that are invaluable to consumers. With a quick e-mail, an Accredited Buyer Representative (ABR) can contact a Certified

Residential Specialist (CRS) about a listing to get more information. Both agents know that they are dealing with a professional at a higher level, even if they've never met before.

The following list outlines NAR-affiliated designations and certifications that may be helpful to you as a home buyer.

- ABR: The Accredited Buyer Representative designation indicates a real estate agent specializing in representing buyers in the real estate transaction. The ABR is conferred by the Real Estate Buyer's Agent Council (REBAC).

- ABRM: The Accredited Buyer Representative Manager, also conferred by REBAC, is designed for those who manage or supervise buyer agents. Holding an ABR designation is a prerequisite for the ABRM, as is the supervision of 25 buyer representation transactions.

- At Home with Diversity: REALTORS® with the At Home with Diversity certification have been trained in and are sensitive to a wide range of cultural issues.

- CRB: The Certified Real Estate Brokerage Manager designation, conferred by the Real Estate Brokerage Managers Council, identifies brokers who have taken an extensive array of courses oriented toward enhancement of brokerage management skills.

- CRS: The Certified Residential Specialist designation by the Council of Residential Specialists denotes an agent who specializes in residential real estate. About 9 percent of the members of NAR have earned this designation.

- GRI: Approximately 18 percent of all REALTORS® have earned the designation Graduate REALTOR® Institute. The

GRI designation identifies REALTORS® who are highly trained in many areas of real estate to better serve and protect their clients.

■ RAA: The Residential Accredited Appraiser designation is for certified residential appraisers whose education and experience exceed state appraisal certification requirements.

■ e-PRO®: The e-PRO® certification identifies real estate professionals who are trained in online marketing and communication technologies, and its graduates are considered Internet professionals.

■ RSPS: The Resort and Second Home Property Specialist (RSPS) certification is for REALTORS® who specialize in marketing, selling, and management of properties for investment, development, retirement, or second homes as a resort, recreational, and/or vacation destination.

As you can see, many of the NAR designations and certifications, conferred by NAR or its institutes, societies, and councils, approach almost graduate levels in terms of training. For more information on the NAR family of designations and certifications, please go to www.REALTOR.org and select the "Education" link.

In addition, there are other designations and certifications that are not affiliated with NAR but are held by numerous real estate agents.

■ SRES: A Senior Real Estate Specialist specializes in senior issues, including financial planning as regards real estate.

■ EBA: An Exclusive Buyer Agent works exclusively with buyers and never represents sellers or participates in dual agency.

- CRP: A Relocation Specialist is a specialist in the relocation process, including family issues, tax and legal issues, appraisals, and corporate relocation policies and issues.

Why Hire a Buyer's Agent?

If you are interested in finding a buyer's agent, visit the web site of the Real Estate Buyer's Agent Council, www.rebac.net. This is the world's largest organization of real estate professionals who focus specifically on representing the real estate buyer in the transaction. Members work as buyer's agents, treating the buyer as a preferred customer. Buyer's agents specialize in assisting buyers with real estate transactions and generally do not take property listings. Many serve as exclusive agents for the buyer. Exclusive buyer's agents can also be found at the National Association of Exclusive Buyer Agents (NAEBA) at www.NAEBA.org.

According to REBAC, a real estate buyer's representative represents the buyer who is purchasing property in a real estate transaction. Research by NAR has shown that when a buyer's representative is used, the prospective buyer finds a home one week faster and examines three more properties than consumers who do not use a buyer's representative.

The buyer's representative works for, and owes fiduciary responsibilities to, the real estate buyer and has the buyer's best interests in mind throughout the entire real estate process. A buyer's representative will:

- Evaluate the specific needs and wants of the buyer and locate properties that fit those specifications.

- Assist buyers in determining the amount that they can afford (prequalify), and show properties in that price range and locale.

- Assist in viewing properties—accompany the buyer on the showings, or preview the properties on behalf of the buyer to ensure that the identified specifications are met.

- Research the selected properties to identify any problems or issues to help the buyer make an informed decision prior to making an offer to purchase the property.

- Advise the buyer on structuring an appropriate offer to purchase the selected property.

- Present the offer to the seller's agent and the seller on the buyer's behalf.

- Negotiate on behalf of the buyer to help obtain the identified property, keeping the buyer's best interests in mind.

- Assist in securing appropriate financing for the selected property.

- Provide a list of potential qualified vendors (e.g., movers, attorneys, carpenters, etc.) if these services are needed.

- Most important, fully represent the buyer throughout the real estate transaction.

(Copyright 2006. Reprinted with permission from REBAC.)

The Buyer Representation Agreement

It is important for the buyer to discuss the buyer's representative's compensation in the initial interview. In many cases it is recommended that the buyer and the buyer's representative agree to the terms of compensation prior to viewing properties, and sign a written agreement reflecting those terms. The agreement should spell out the responsibilities of both parties throughout the real estate process.

In some states, legislation has been enacted to protect the buyer to the point that, absent a written agreement, the buyer's representative represents the buyer throughout the real estate transaction. Consult your agent for complete details when you begin the purchase process.

A buyer's agent who is working specifically for you can help you find a home beyond the confines of homes listed by other agents in the local MLS. He can help you with new homes, for-sale-by-owner homes, and homes that he learns about through networking that are coming on the market but are not listed yet.

Hiring Your Agent

If you've never bought a home before, or you are moving to a new area where you don't know anyone, you may wonder what is the best way to go about finding the right real estate agent. One way is to ask for referrals from people who have recently been in a similar situation as you. And while experience plays an important role, the enthusiasm of a newer real estate professional can't be discounted. The important thing is to get the kind of service and support that's right for you.

If you are not sure how to go about hiring an agent, here are some recommendations:

Interview a Minimum of Three Agents

According to NAR, most buyers choose the first agent they meet or the first agent that is recommended to them, so make sure that person is in tune with your experience level and is someone who has resources to help you get a loan and find the right home, and the experience and support from his/her company to make your transaction go as smoothly as possible. Possible sources to find the right agent are:

- Asking family and friends for referrals.
- Meeting agents at open houses and other events.
- Meeting agents online or through other advertising.

You may find you already know an agent who is also a friend or family member. While it may seem like a great idea to hire this person, remember that your personal relationship stands the chance of being affected by the businesslike negotiations of buying.

Look for Professionalism

Agents can work full- or part-time, but you want a professional, someone who is up to date in the market, has the latest education or continuing education, and takes her responsibilities seriously enough to be available full-time. There are too many changes in the law, the local market, and mortgage loans to risk your most important transaction on someone who isn't committed to you.

You also want someone who is continually updating his own skills as well as his education. While some continuing education may be required for licensure, find out if the agent has gone beyond the minimum requirement to seek out other certifications or designations. Be sure to ask what is the latest skill the agent has added to his toolbox. Has he recently taken a technology course? Attended a class on architecture? The answer might be very revealing.

Evaluate the Answers According to Your Needs

While you want an agent who is compatible with you and your family, other attributes may be just as important, if not more so. Your agent should:

- *Be knowledgeable*. Your agent should know the benefits and problems of buying in the neighborhood you want, as well as the type of home you want. For example, a condominium community offers a different lifestyle and homeowner responsibilities than single-family home ownership. Buying from a builder requires a more professional approach than buying from a homeowner, where the negotiations are likely to be more personal.

- *Be a good educator*. Your agent should be able to explain what you need to know to buy a home, so that you make the fewest mistakes possible and get as close to meeting your goals as possible. A reputable agent will show you housing inventory within your qualifying range. She will explain the importance of prequalifying with a good lender so your offer will be more seriously considered by sellers. A good agent will show you how to buy the best home for your money where you want to live.

- *Be capable.* Your agent should be able to meet your special needs as a buyer. First-time buyers have more need for assistance and attention than transferees who have packed and moved a dozen times. Families with young children have different priorities than seniors, who may have financial aspects to their selling and buying that require special expertise. An experienced agent should be in tune with the life cycles of consumers and be able to provide the services they need.

- *Be a good communicator.* Your agent should keep you informed of the latest listings, interest rate alerts, market conditions, red flags, and other data that could impact your transaction. Frequent communication by e-mail, phone, or fax is desirable.

- *Be experienced.* Experience is relative. One agent may have years of experience in selling real estate, but not in the neighborhood or type of home you wish to buy. A new agent, on the other hand, may not have much experience in sales, but she may bowl you over with enthusiasm and energy, or he may have the Internet communication skills to send you information in the manner you want. Judge an agent's experience on how you prefer they work with you as a home buyer.

Choose the Best Candidate

By the time you interview at least three agents, you'll have a better idea of which agent is most likely to meet your needs. If you don't feel comfortable, keep looking!

Don't be tempted to hire several agents, thinking you will cover more ground. That may be true if you are looking across several counties, but not if you are looking in the same general area. The other agents will find out sooner or later. Agents network and tell each other about their prospects, hoping to hear about houses that haven't hit the market yet. If they think they are working with a customer who isn't loyal, they may terminate the relationship.

The nature of representation is changing. Buyers are more frequently entering into contracts of representation with agents because of the considerable protections and advantages they afford. When you decide on one agent, empower that agent to go to work for you.

To have a good working relationship, be as honest as you can about your needs, wants, and abilities. Be flexible in allowing your agent to show you ideas you haven't thought about. Financing alternatives or a different neighborhood or type of home may meet your needs better than the ones you imagined. Be willing to speak up when you aren't comfortable with the way a home search or a negotiation is headed. Give the agent the chance to make things right when they go wrong.

Questions to Ask When Choosing an Agent

1. How long have you been in residential real estate sales? Is this your full-time job? (While experience is no guarantee of skill, in real estate, like many other professions, most knowledge is learned on the job.)

2. What designations do you hold? (Designations such as GRI and CRS, which require that real estate professionals take additional, specialized real estate training, are held by only about a quarter of real estate practitioners.)

3. How many homes did you and your company sell last year?

4. How many days did it take you to sell the average home? How did that compare to the overall market?

5. How close to the initial asking prices of the homes you sold were the final sale prices?

6. What types of specific marketing systems and approaches will you use to sell my home? (Look for someone who has aggressive, innovative approaches, not just someone who's going to put a sign in the yard and hope for the best.)

7. Will you represent me exclusively, or will you represent both the buyer and the seller in the transaction? (While it's usually legal to represent both parties in a transaction, it's important to understand where the practitioner's obligations lie. A good practitioner will explain the agency relationship to you and describe the rights of each party. It's also possible to hire a practitioner to represent you exclusively.)

Questions to Ask When Choosing an Agent *(Continued)*

8. Can you recommend service providers who can assist me in obtaining a mortgage, making repairs on my home, and other things I need done? (Keep in mind here that real estate professionals should generally recommend more than one provider and should tell you if they receive any compensation from any provider.)

9. What type of support and supervision does your brokerage office provide to you? (Having resources, such as in-house support staff, access to a real estate attorney, or assistance with technology, can help a real estate professional sell homes.)

10. What's your business philosophy? (While there's no right answer to this question, the response will help you assess what's important to the real estate practitioner—fast sales, service, and so on—and determine how closely the practitioner's goals and business emphasis mesh with your own.)

11. How will you keep me informed about the progress of my transaction? How frequently? Using what media? (Again, this is not a question with a correct answer, but one that reflects your desires. Do you want updates twice a week or don't want to be bothered unless there's a hot prospect? Do you prefer phone, e-mail, or a personal visit?)

12. Could you please give me the names and phone numbers of your three most recent clients?

(Copyright 2006. Reprinted with permission from REALTOR® Magazine Online.)

Understanding Representation

It's important to understand what legal responsibilities your real estate salesperson has to you and to other parties in the transactions. Ask your salesperson to explain what type of agency relationships are available to you if you elect to work with him or her and with the brokerage company.

1. *Seller's representative* (also known as a *listing agent* or *seller's agent*). A seller's agent is hired by and represents the seller. All fiduciary duties are owed to the seller. The agency relationship usually is created by a listing contract.

2. *Subagent*. A subagent owes the same fiduciary duties to the agent's principal as the agent does. Subagency usually arises when a cooperating sales associate from another brokerage, who is not representing the buyer as a buyer's representative or operating in a nonagency relationship, shows property to a buyer. In such a case, the subagent works *with* the buyer as a customer but owes fiduciary duties to the listing broker and the seller. Although a subagent cannot assist the buyer in any way that would be detrimental to the seller, a buyer-customer can expect to be treated honestly by the subagent. It is important that subagents fully explain their duties to buyers.

3. *Buyer's representative* (also known as a *buyer's agent*). A buyer's rep is a real estate licensee who is hired by prospective buyers to represent them in a real estate transaction. The buyer's rep works in the buyer's best interest throughout the transaction and owes fiduciary du-

ties to the buyer. The buyer can pay the licensee directly through a negotiated fee, or the buyer's rep may be paid by the seller or by a commission split with the listing broker.

4. *Disclosed dual agent.* Dual agency is a relationship in which the brokerage firm represents both the buyer and the seller in the same real estate transaction. Dual agency relationships do not carry with them all of the traditional fiduciary duties to the clients. Instead, dual agents owe limited fiduciary duties. Because of the potential for conflicts of interest in a dual agency relationship, it's vital that all parties give their informed consent. In many states, this consent must be in writing. Disclosed dual agency, in which both the buyer and the seller are told that the agent is representing both of them and both consent to such an arrangement, is legal in most states.

5. *Designated agent* (also called, among other things, *appointed agency*). This is a brokerage practice that allows the managing broker to designate which licensees in the brokerage will act as an agent of the seller and which will act as an agent of the buyer. Designated agency avoids the problem of creating a dual agency relationship for licensees at the brokerage. The designated agents give their clients full representation, with all of the attendant fiduciary duties. The broker still has the responsibility of supervising both groups of licensees and may be considered a dual agent depending on state law.

6. *Nonagency relationship* (called, among other things, a *transaction broker* or *facilitator*). Some states permit a real estate licensee to have a type of nonagency relationship with a

consumer. These relationships vary considerably from state to state, both as to the duties owed to the consumer and the name used to describe them. Very generally, the duties owed to the consumer in a nonagency relationship are less than the complete, traditional fiduciary duties of an agency relationship.

(Copyright 2006. Reprinted with permission from REALTOR® Magazine Online.)

Agency Disclosure

Most states require real estate agents to disclose to consumers if they have a relationship with the other party in a potential transaction. For example, if you attend an open house and ask questions about the house, the agent may not be obligated to tell you that he represents the seller. But if you express interest in buying the house, then the agent must disclose his relationship with the seller. If you want him to represent you, you will most likely have to enter a dual agency relationship where the agent is representing both you and the seller (unless the state allows transactional brokerage). Both you and the seller must be informed of the dual agency and consent to the relationship. But let's say you decide not to buy that house. You can then hire the agent as your exclusive agent to find you a home.

Negotiating Commissions

In most cases, the buyer's broker is paid out of the listing broker's commission, so it will not be necessary for you to negotiate a commission. When the listing broker enters the listing into the MLS, he offers a cooperating fee to selling brokers, which could include subagents and/or buyer's brokers, to help him get the listing sold. Because the listing broker is offering your agent part of his commission, it is not necessary for you to pay your broker.

Of course, this provision is only good for properties listed in the MLS where listing brokers have agreed to pay cooperating fees. What about builders' homes or for-sale-by-owner homes? How does the buyer's broker get paid?

If you want your buyer's broker to show you unlisted homes, you will most likely be asked to sign an agreement, which includes the guarantee that you will pay his commission instead of the seller. If the sales contract specifies the payment of the buyer's broker fee by the seller, you won't be required to bring extra money to the table. If the contract does not, you will be required to pay your broker's fee when you close on the property.

Finally, your broker has a policy about commissions, and your salesperson or associate broker may not be able to accept negotiations that deviate from company policy.

CHAPTER 3

Planning Your Home Buying Adventure

Congratulations! You're about to start on one of the most exciting adventures of your life—finding and buying a home.

To plan your home buying experience for the greatest thrills and the fewest bumps, you have a lot of factors to consider.

What Do You Want in a Home?

When you first decide to buy a home, it's tempting to go to the Internet and start looking at advertised properties, but soon you'll find yourself gazing wistfully at homes that you can't afford, that aren't in the area you want, or that otherwise don't meet your needs.

Instead, start with a list of features you would really like to have. Because of today's emphasis on luxury amenities in almost every price range, you'll be surprised at what you really can afford. Homes may cost a lot more than you thought, or they may be less expensive than you planned.

If you live in an area where you can have an easy choice between urban and suburban living, the options are even more exciting because you can choose a home that suits your lifestyle as well as your finances.

Here are some quick questions that may help you narrow your focus so you can zero in on the right home.

Why Do You Want to Buy a Home?

Everyone should be able to answer this question. If you're like most home buyers you may want more space. Need a studio for your paints and hobbies? Need a home office? Want a yard for your children or pets?

Your answers will tell you something about your space requirements as well as the number of rooms you might need. While you might be happy setting your computer up on the dining room table in your apartment, you may not want to continue doing that in your new home. Think about why you're going to the trouble and expense of moving and what problems a new home will solve. Understanding your motivation should lead you to the next question.

Where Do You Want to Live?

You may want to live near your family or friends and/or within an easy commute of your employer. You'll want to visit those neighborhoods that meet your criteria to figure out if there is one area that suits you better in terms of costs, types of housing, space, and amenities.

Neighborhoods don't tend to be eclectic, so most homes will be fairly comparable to other homes in the neighborhood. Ask your agent where you can get the most space with the neighborhood amenities you want.

What Characteristics Do You Want in Your Home?

According to the *2004 NAR Profile of Buyers' Home Feature Preferences*, compiled by NAR, home buyers prefer to live large, but don't let your eyes get too big. The 2004 statistics indicated that less than half of first-time home buyers got all the features they deemed "somewhat or very important" in the home they purchased. Repeat buyers did a little better at 58 percent. Go ahead and make your wish list as big as you want, but be prepared to compromise.

10 Tips for First-Time Home Buyers

1. *Be picky, but don't be unrealistic.* There is no perfect home.

2. *Do your homework before you start looking.* Decide specifically what features you want in a home and which are most important to you.

3. *Get your finances in order.* Review your credit report and be sure you have enough money to cover your down payment and your closing costs.

4. *Don't wait to get a loan.* Talk to a lender and get prequalified for a mortgage before you start looking.

5. *Don't ask too many people for opinions.* It will drive you crazy. Select one or two people to turn to if you feel you need a second opinion.

6. *Decide when you could move.* When is your lease up? Are you allowed to sublet? How tight is the rental market in your area?

7. *Think long-term.* Are you looking for a starter house with the idea of moving up in a few years or do you hope to stay in this home longer? This decision may dictate what type of home you'll buy as well as the type of mortgage terms that suit you best.

8. *Don't let yourself be "house poor."* If you max yourself out to buy the biggest home you can afford, you'll have no money left for maintenance or decoration or to save money for other financial goals.

9. *Don't be naïve.* Insist on a home inspection and, if possible, get a warranty from the seller to cover defects within one year.

10. *Get help.* Consider hiring a REALTOR® as a buyer's representative. Unlike a listing agent, whose first duty is to the seller, a buyer's representative is working only for you. And often buyer's reps are paid out of the seller's commission payment.

(Copyright 2006. Reprinted with permission from REALTOR® Magazine Online.)

Your chances of finding more of the features and amenities you want are greater in a new home, but your costs will be greater, too. Some features will be obsolete, and that is something to consider in the home you're buying, particularly an older home. For example, homes built before the 1960s tend to have closed-away kitchens because homemakers didn't want their efforts to show. They wanted to appear like magic with dinner on a tray, wearing their pearls and heels. Modern home buyers want kitchens open to the family room because both parents may work, and both may prepare dinner together. Breakfast and dinner, from preparation to serving, is an ideal time to visit while the rest of the family is gathered nearby at the breakfast bar or in front of the TV.

Certain features have become so ubiquitous that it is almost impossible to sell a home unless they're included. These include air-conditioning, central heating, and garages, yet many homes built before the 1970s don't have these features. The largest inventory of homes are those built before 1980, so be prepared to compromise on a few luxuries, or consider home improvements when you shop for homes of that age.

Think about how important it is to have certain features and amenities. Three out of four buyers who got what they said they wanted bought single-story homes with nine-foot ceilings, one or more fireplaces, walk-in master closets, downstairs master bedroom and baths, central air, cable/satellite, and patios. Half purchased homes with monitored security; sitting rooms in the master bedroom; cathedral ceilings; fenced, sprinklered, and decked yards; oversized garage; attics; and more.

What is significant is whether they were willing to pay more for a home to get the features they wanted. For instance, 24 percent of the respondents said they were willing to pay more for nine-foot ceilings; 40 percent of the respondents were willing to pay more for a home that had air filtration systems; 66 percent were willing to pay more for a home with a walk-in closet; and 54 percent were willing to pay more for a home with a patio.

What Activities Will You Be Able to Do?

Imagine yourself living in your new home, doing daily activities. Be sure to include how you like to eat, sleep, relax, entertain, and work.

It sounds simple enough, but choosing a home based on how you like to eat isn't a bad way to do it. If you like to graze in the kitchen, think about a breakfast bar or an island where you can pull up stools for a bite of cake. If you like to entertain with dinner and conversation, you'll want a formal dining room, even if it's not fancy. If you have a family, you might want a breakfast room where you can serve breakfast and lunch and watch your kids play in the backyard while you have a cup of coffee.

How do you like to sleep and dress in the morning? Do you want a lot of room to spread out with a king-size bed and a sitting area for reading or late-night TV? How much time do you need to get ready for work in the morning? Can you share a bath with your spouse, or would your relationship thrive on separate vanities, tub, and shower?

How far is your commute? Does the layout of your house help you as far as giving you time with the family before your hop your train or back out of the drive?

How many parking spaces do you need? Can you swing a two- or three-car garage so you can store the bikes indoors, too? Maybe you don't own a car but could use a little storage space?

Can you work at home? Many telecommuters use home offices not only to maximize productivity but to start home businesses that allow them to take considerable deductions at tax time, virtually subsidizing the additional costs of having a home with a home office space.

Next, think about what it's like to come home. Do you like to cook? Do you prepare meals with your spouse and perhaps need a more generous work area? Will the gourmet cook need a lot of storage for fancy cookware and serving pieces?

How do you like to relax? What are your hobbies? Do your activities require special features such as lots of ventilation for painting or ceramics, or bookshelves and storage for books and collectibles? Do you exercise at home, and would you like to have your own equipment?

How do you like to entertain family and guests—with parties, intimate dinners, gaming nights with pool tables and poker chips? Will you need a second living area such as a family den? Will you want a formal living room or would you prefer the laid-back atmosphere of a game room or media room? Is a built-in entertainment center important to you?

How many people are in your household and what are their preferences? Do you need a private suite and retreat for an in-law, teenager, or caregiver? What about a basement living area for your son's garage band? Where do you want the master bedroom situated—near young children's bedrooms for safekeeping or in a private wing of your own? What are your attitudes about sharing baths and bedrooms among the children? Will you need an extra bedroom to use as flexible space or a bonus room?

All of these considerations contribute to the cost and maintenance of your home. Unless you are a multizillionaire, the chances are good you won't be able to get everything you want in any home, regardless of cost, but you may get more than you ever dreamed.

In working with buyers, NAR found in its *2004 Profile of Buyers' Home Feature Preferences* that the following are the most desired home features:

- Central air-conditioning—73 percent.
- Walk-in closet, master bedroom—51 percent.
- Bedroom on main level—42 percent.
- Patio—41 percent.
- Oversize garage—41 percent.
- Cable/satellite TV–ready—40 percent.
- Fencing—37 percent.
- Separate shower in master bath—36 percent.
- Porch—34 percent.
- Eat-in kitchen—32 percent.

The bottom line is you'll likely have to compromise on something—location, size, and/or amenities. But don't let that discourage you. Many people have purchased a home they had no idea they were going to buy, simply because it had one *amazing* feature they couldn't live without. So if that stunning view or fabulous bath is worth it, your compromises will seem less important.

Here are some other compromises you might think about:

- If you were to buy an existing home in a highly desirable neighborhood, do you think you could compromise on an old-fashioned floor plan and lack of separate vanities for the time being in order to get that premium location? You can always remodel the bathroom later when you have more money.

- Could you live with not having a dog as a companion in order to enjoy the spectacular views of the city from your high-rise apartment? If you really want a pet, there's always a way to compromise. You can hire a pet-walking service. Or you could buy a house with a yard.

- Do you want a brand-new home with the latest décor, state-of-the-art appliances and electronics, and a big yard? To get all that, you might have to make a longer commute to your job. Are you willing to spend more time in your car or on a train, or could you change your job to work some from home?

As you can see, there are always ways to get what you want. Just remember to include the extra costs in your monthly budget.

Speaking of budgets, creating one is the first major step you need to take to buy a home.

10 Steps to Prepare for Home Ownership

1. Decide how much home you can afford. Generally, you can afford a home equal in value to between two and three times your gross income.

2. Develop a wish list of what you'd like your home to have. Then prioritize the features on your list.

3. Select three or four neighborhoods you'd like to live in. Consider items such as schools, recreational facilities, area expansion plans, and safety.

4. Determine if you have enough saved to cover your down payment and closing costs. Closing costs, including taxes, attorney's fees, and transfer fees, average between 2 percent and 7 percent of the home price.

5. Get your credit in order. Obtain a copy of your credit report.

6. Determine how large a mortgage you can qualify for. Also explore different loan options and decide what's best for you.

7. Organize all the documentation a lender will need to preapprove you for a loan.

8. Do research to determine if you qualify for any special mortgage or down payment assistance programs.

9. Calculate the costs of home ownership, including property taxes, insurance, maintenance, and association fees, if applicable.

10. Find an experienced REALTOR® who can help you through the process.

(Copyright 2006. Reprinted with permission from REALTOR® Magazine Online.)

How Much Home Should You Buy?

When you are choosing a home of your own, you naturally want to get as much house for the money as possible. The trick is to buy as much as you can reasonably afford without becoming house poor.

It's tempting to buy at the top of your range because rising appreciation has made it profitable for many home buyers to sell their homes and trade up after only a few years. If they can buy in a more desirable area, assuring higher and quicker resale, it's worth the risk.

But consider the costs. To buy and sell the same home, you will have to pay a number of professional fees including closing costs, lender fees, real estate agency fees, attorney's fees, movers, and more. From that standpoint, it makes more sense to buy as much house as possible to take you through several life cycles—better jobs, bigger family, and so on—and stay put for a few years until your appreciation can not only cover your transaction costs but allow you to buy your next home with more money down, so you can minimize higher house payments while enjoying more space and amenities.

Many agents will advise you that since you will trade up eventually, you may as well buy your trade-up home now. You'll save money in new financing costs, closing costs, moving costs, commissions, and marketing fees, plus the awful hassle of moving. There is also the great unknown to consider. What will the housing market be like in a few years? No one knows. You might not be able to buy as nice a home then as you can now. All things considered, it's better to buy the most home now.

But there's another point of view. You may have other goals, such as improving your home, buying furniture or a car, bringing children into the family, taking vacations, covering medical expenses, paying off student loans, making investments, building cash reserves, and much more.

Leading financial advisers argue that owning a home is only one way to build wealth. They think in terms of return on investment versus risk. As shown earlier, homes offer a fair hedge against inflation, but that is about the most you can expect from them as investments.

Rising home values can be brought down to earth by maintenance costs, property taxes, homeowner's insurance, repairs, and local market fluctuations. But home ownership offers many more financial benefits than renting, so a financial planner will agree that you do need to buy a home. She will insist that you diversify your assets by creating or adding to a portfolio of cash reserves and other investments. This risk-managed approach positions you to do three things well: Handle reversals in your finances such as a job loss, pursue other goals such as saving for retirement or starting a family, and build wealth by investing in securities, all while enjoying occupancy in a nice home.

All the arguments from both sides are sound, so the solution lies in how to have your cake and eat it, too. That means buying the most home possible without becoming house poor. How you accomplish this goal depends on several things—the information you provide to the lender, which loan you choose, how long you plan to stay in your home, and what your other financial goals are.

How Big a Mortgage Can I Afford?

Not only does owning a home give you a haven for yourself and your family, it makes great financial sense, too. This calculation assumes a 28 percent income tax bracket. If your bracket is higher, your savings will be, too.

Rent: _____

Multiplier: × 1.32

Mortgage payment: _____

Because of tax deductions, you can make a mortgage payment—including taxes and insurance—that is approximately one-third larger than your current rent payment and end up with the same amount of income.

For more help, use Fannie Mae's online mortgage calculators at http://www.fanniemae.com/homebuyers/calculators/index.jhtml?p=Resources&s=Calculators

(Copyright 2006. Reprinted with permission from REALTOR® Magazine Online.)

What Are Your Financial Goals Besides Buying a Home?

You have other goals besides buying a home. What are they? Do you want to have children? Do you want to build wealth? Save for retirement or retire early?

Baby makes three, but three into two incomes doesn't go as far. Count on spending up to $25,000 on a child just in the first two years. That will be more difficult if one of you stays home or works shorter hours in order to parent.

Do you want to build wealth? Start investing or add to your investments? The authors of *The Millionaire Next Door* (Simon & Schuster), PhD's Thomas J. Stanley and William D. Danko, advise that you spend no more than twice your household income on a mortgage. If that leaves you safe financially, but short on a stylish home, you can compromise. You don't have to spend as much as the lender guidelines allow (28 percent of gross income), nor do you have to tighten your belt as much as the authors suggest. Find out how much home you can qualify for and simply inform your agent what price range you're comfortable with.

Living in style is about more than having a big, expensive trophy house. It's about being able to meet all your financial goals comfortably. And with the right compromises, discipline, and foresight, you can do both.

Eight Steps to Getting Your Finances in Order

1. *Develop a family budget.* Instead of budgeting what you'd like to spend, use receipts to create a budget for what you actually spent over the last six months. One advantage of this approach is that it factors in unexpected expenses, such as car repairs, illnesses, and so on, as well as predictable costs such as rent.

2. *Reduce your debt.* Generally speaking, lenders look for a total debt load of no more than 36 percent of income. Since this figure includes your mortgage, which typically ranges between 25 percent and 28 percent of income, you need to get the rest of your installment debt—car loans, student loans, revolving balances on credit cards—down to between 8 percent and 10 percent of your total income.

3. *Get a handle on expenses.* You probably know how much you spend on rent and utilities, but little expenses add up. Try writing down *everything* you spend for one month. You'll probably see some great ways to save.

4. *Increase your income.* It may be necessary to take on a second, part-time job to get your income at a high enough level to qualify for the home you want.

5. *Save for a down payment.* Although it is possible to get a mortgage with only 5 percent down—or even less in some cases—you can usually get a better rate and a lower overall cost if you put down more. Shoot for saving a 20 percent down payment.

6. *Create a house fund.* Don't just plan on saving whatever's left toward a down payment. Instead decide on a certain amount a month you want to save, then put it away as you pay your monthly bills.

7. *Keep your job.* While you don't need to be in the same job forever to qualify, having a job for less than two years may mean you have to pay a higher interest rate.

8. *Establish a good credit history.* Get a credit card and make payments by the due date. Do the same for all your other bills. Pay off the entire balance promptly.

(Copyright 2006. Reprinted with permission from REALTOR® Magazine Online.)

Consider Your Finances

There are many financial factors that apply when you consider owning a home, but only a few are significant to a lender: your employment history, how much of a down payment you plan to make, what your gross income is versus your debts, and your credit history (payment history).

But you need to think bigger than a mortgage loan. You need to think about how you are going to meet your other monthly obligations. Some include:

- Monthly payment of principal, interest, homeowner's insurance, and property taxes.
- Home operating costs (utilities, landscaping costs, homeowners association dues, repairs, home improvement).
- Transportation costs.
- Revolving credit card accounts.
- Other monthly costs (student loans, car payments, electronics, phones, etc.).
- Savings and retirement—401(k)s, investment accounts, savings accounts.

These are just the basic monthly costs you will have, and you may have others. Make a budget that includes more than the minimum payments to these obligations. Think about the utility costs in a larger home, so you can estimate what you'll be spending.

Budget Basics Worksheet

The first step in getting yourself in financial shape to buy a home is to know what you make and what you spend now. List your income and expenses below.

Income	
Take-Home Pay/All Family Members	
Child Support/Alimony	
Pension/Social Security	
Disability/Other Insurance	
Interest/Dividends	
Other	
Total Income	
Expenses	
Rent/Mortgage	
Life Insurance	
Health/Disability Insurance	
Vehicle Insurance	
Homeowner's or Other Insurance	
Car Payments	
Other Loan Payments	
Savings/Pension Contribution	
Utilities	
Credit Card Payments	

(Continued)

Budget Basics Worksheet (Continued)	
Car Upkeep	
Clothing	
Personal Care Products	
Groceries	
Food Prepared Outside the Home	
Medical/Dental/Prescriptions	
Household Goods	
Recreation/Entertainment	
Child Care	
Education	
Charitable Donations	
Miscellaneous	
Total Expenses	
Remaining Income After Expenses	

(Copyright 2006. Reprinted with permission from REALTOR® Magazine Online.)

Ask about Utilities

If you are coming from an apartment with all bills paid, you might not have any idea what utilities truly cost. Ask your agent to ask the seller for an average of the utility bills during the most demanding months (summer and winter) so you can get an idea of what you'll be spending to operate your home.

Your water, gas, and electricity bills can vary greatly according to how much yard you have; whether the seller has updated the furnace, insulated the attic, and taken other actions to conserve energy; how many electronic devices you have; your personal habits (do you turn lights off when you leave the room?); and many other factors.

What Your Lender Needs to Know

Lenders make the decision to grant a loan based on avoiding as much risk as possible in their investment, as well as on guidelines to ensure loans can be resold on the secondary market. The amount of your loan will be determined by four basic criteria—income, assets, debts, and the interest rate that you can lock in. Insurer guidelines suggest that you not spend more than 28 percent of your income on your mortgage and that your debts not exceed 36 to 38 percent of your income.

Lenders qualify income to include gross yearly pay, including overtime, part-time, seasonal pay, commissions, bonuses, and tips. Also included are dividends from investments, business income, pension or Social Security income, veteran's benefits, alimony, and child support.

But do you really want to count your nonsalaried income? Think about it. Is overtime really a reliable source of income? Do you want to force yourself to work overtime every year to pay for your house? If you don't, don't include overtime in your income statement. What about child support? Has your check been late or failed to arrive at all? And as far as dividends go, you could be reinvesting them to make your stock account grow. You don't need them as income to buy a house.

See what kind of a loan you can qualify for based simply on your yearly salary without these extra bonuses. If you easily meet a 30-year fixed rate mortgage in a range you're comfortable with, you know you have some wiggle room.

Limiting your income statement to your salary can give you bargaining room later. If you decide to buy a home that is a little outside the lender guidelines, you'll have other income the lender can consider, or you can choose a less expensive loan product.

Using the Lender's Loan Products to Leverage More House

A 30-year fixed rate mortgage is the standard of the loan industry, but is it necessarily the right product for you? The answer may lie in two things—how long you plan on occupying your new home and whether you are choosing a home slightly out of your salary-only income range.

If you are a first-time home buyer, the odds are that you'll be in your home for about four years. If you are a second home buyer, plan on about 7 to 12 years of occupancy. The shorter time you occupy your home, the less time you have to build equity.

Equity equals ownership. If you are not planning to stay in your house long, pay as little in financing costs as possible. In such case you would pay more for a fixed rate loan in interest payments than you need to. A better alternative might be a hybrid loan which has a fixed rate for a short period of time, up to 10 years. After that, the loan resets to an adjustable rate, but by that time, you will have sold the home and paid off the loan. You can also save money by not paying points, and by financing as much of the closing costs as possible.

Here's why. The longer you owe money to a lender, the higher the risk is for the lender. A 30-year fixed rate loan is a low-risk loan for you, because the rate never changes, but it's a higher risk for lenders because they could possibly make more money charging higher interest down the road.

To really hedge your bet, save the difference every month between what you would have paid on a 30-year note and what you are paying on an interest-only or adjustable rate loan. Invest that difference where your financial adviser suggests you'll get the most return—a CD, mutual funds, cash management account, or paying down the principal on your note.

But even this isn't a risk-free strategy. If interest rates are rising, you might end up paying more for your home than you can comfortably afford if interest rates reset from a relatively low fixed rate to a much higher adjustable rate. You'll know when your adjustable rate resets by the terms of your loan—a 1/1 adjusts in one year, a 3/1 adjusts in three years, a 5/1 adjusts in five years, and so on. If you are not certain you will like your new loan rate once it resets, you might be more comfortable with a fixed rate loan, but the trade-off may be buying a smaller or more modest home.

If interest rates are rising too fast, take heart. One day, you may be able to refinance your loan in order to lower your payments. When the time comes, take advantage of consolidating your loan into a shorter term, such as a 20-year note, to offset refinancing costs. (For more about mortgage options, see Chapter 4.)

Keep in mind that buying a home is part of an overall financial strategy that includes investment, home appreciation, and savings. Not saving any money increases your risk. Even the most bullish financial adviser will suggest that you diversify your holdings. That means making sure you have enough to put toward other purposes besides buying a home.

What you buy, one day you'll sell. Perhaps you want to cash in on a rising market to get in and out of a property quickly. Tax laws favor selling real estate after five years of ownership and two years of occupancy, and a rising market has allowed many to move up to more expensive homes or take their profits from their first home and invest it in two properties, and so on.

When interest rates are low, it's tempting to buy a little bit more than you can comfortably afford. But should you? That depends on your tolerance for risk.

What You Should Know About House Payments

Fixed rates don't mean house payments never change. This is especially useful information for you to know if you are a first-time home buyer. In a fixed rate mortgage only the mortgage rate and the required principal and interest payment are fixed—insurance and property taxes can and usually do increase every year.

Don't Be Overtaxed by Property Taxes

One frequently overlooked cost to homeowners is property taxes. This is an area where your agent can be helpful. As you look at homes, you may visit different municipalities or areas within the city that have higher or lower tax rates. When you are considering a home, ask what the tax rate is for that area. Keep in mind that the homeowner may be paying a much lower amount in taxes because of when they bought the home.

Tax authorities base taxes on current market value, but they usually have consumer protection rules in place that prevent them from raising property taxes at exorbitant rates. The reason that the homeowner's tax bill isn't relevant is because they most likely paid a different price for the home than you are going to pay. As you figure monthly payments on your calculator, be sure to add what the monthly tax assessment is likely to be on the amount you paid, and then count on the local tax authority to raise it the following year.

While most tax authorities will allow you to protest your tax bill, it will be hard to prove that what you paid isn't market value, so be sure to ask your agent to provide you with annual *comparables* (remember the CMA?) at tax protesting time (within a few weeks or months of receiving your annual assessment) so you can keep your taxes as low as possible.

Sometimes buyers are surprised to learn that their taxes go up significantly the second calendar year they occupy the home. In addition they discover that the lender may not be escrowing the correct amount! That's because the lender is working from the previous year's tax assessment, which doesn't reflect the new price you just paid for the home. Your new purchase price resets the assessment and may include appreciation, too. You'll get a notice in the mail of your new assessment, but the lender isn't notified until the tax bill comes due. If the lender doesn't have enough set aside in escrow, you will be billed the difference until that year's taxes are caught up. As soon as you get your new assessment, calculate what you think you will owe in taxes for the remainder of the year, and include it in your mortgage payment under "additional escrow" so you won't be caught short.

Homeowner's Insurance

In Texas and California a couple of years ago, many homeowners experienced a 45 percent increase in insurance premiums due to heavy losses by certain underwriters in the state. Carriers with national policies spread those costs throughout the nation, making rate changes less obvious, but homeowners are always vulnerable to annual changes in premium rates. When some policies renew, homeowners may be told that coverage for some items that they thought were included is now optional, and can only be included at a higher cost or through a separate policy rider. This is true of mold coverage, for example.

An experienced real estate agent can help you in the following ways:

- When you figure principal, interest, taxes, and insurance (commonly referred to as PITI), or use the lender's estimate, your agent will remind you that the PITI is calculated on what the current seller is paying in taxes this year, and that the new assessment will be based on the new sales price that you paid for the property.

- Your agent is aware of property tax laws for your city and county, as well as their current rates, and should keep you informed. However, be sure to ask about these important regulations.

- Your agent knows your area's ceiling on tax rate increases so you can be informed of the maximum possible hikes that might occur for the next couple of years if home prices continue to rise.

- Your agent should be informed on insurance issues that affect your state and will be ready with alternative sources if your insurer will not insure you.

- Your agent should know which companies are insuring in your area, and which ones aren't writing homeowner policies.

- Your agent will offer to supply current comparables so you'll know where your property stands in any given market.

Five Things to Understand about Homeowner's Insurance

1. *Look for exclusions to coverage.* For example, most insurance policies do not cover flood or earthquake damage as a standard item. These coverages must be bought separately.

2. *Look for dollar limitations on claims.* Even if you are covered for a risk, there may a limit on how much the insurer will pay. For example, many policies limit the amount paid for stolen jewelry unless items are insured separately.

3. *Understand replacement cost.* If your home is destroyed, you'll receive money to replace it only to the maximum of your coverage, so be sure your insurance is sufficient. This means that if your home is insured for $150,000 and it costs $180,000 to replace it, you'll only receive $150,000.

4. *Understand actual cash value.* If you choose not to replace your home when it's destroyed, you'll receive replacement cost, less depreciation. This is called actual cash value.

5. *Understand liability.* Generally your homeowner's insurance covers you for accidents that happen to other people on your property, including medical care, court costs, and awards by the court. However, there is usually an upper limit to the amount of coverage provided. Be sure that it's sufficient if you have significant assets.

The Essential Checklist

REALTOR® Magazine Online has prepared a house hunting checklist for agents to give their buyers. The list is designed to be flexible, so use it to help you narrow your selections in types and conditions of homes, location, and amenities. Feel free to add comments if you feel more strongly about a feature than "wants" or "don't wants." Some features are absolute must-haves, while others are absolute deal breakers!

Share the list with your agent and stay open to new ideas. He will have information that will enlighten you to realities and possibilities you might not know about.

Feel free to add your own suggestions. This list, for example, doesn't include a spot for a private pool in the exterior section, but it does include a swimming pool in the community/neighborhood section. For some, a private pool in the backyard is a must-have family amenity. For others, pools are maintenance headaches and insurance liabilities they want to avoid at all costs.

Another area that could use more input from you is how much green space you want around you. Be sure to specify how much yard you want or don't want, and how you would like to maintain what's there. This can tell your agent a lot about your lifestyle needs, storage, and maintenance obligations.

Your Property Wish List

While your opinions on the type of home you want to own may change during the home buying process, use this easy checklist to help you prioritize and make the shopping process less time consuming.

1. How close do you need to be to:

   (a) public transportation _____

   (b) schools _____

   (c) airport _____

   (d) expressway _____

   (e) neighborhood shopping _____

   (f) other _____

2. What neighborhoods would you prefer?

3. What school systems do you want to be near?

4. What architectural style(s) of home do you prefer?

5. Do you want a one-story or two-story house?

6. How old a home would you consider?

7. How much repair or renovation would you be willing to do?

8. Do you have special facilities or needs that your home must meet?

9. Do you require a fenced yard or other amenities for your pets?

(Continued)

Your Property Wish List (Continued)

10. Prioritize each of these options:

	Must have	Would prefer
Yard (at least _____)		
Garage (size: _____)		
Patio/deck		
Pool		
Bedrooms (number: _____)		
Bathrooms (number: _____)		
Family room		
Formal living room		
Formal dining room		
Eat-in kitchen		
Laundry room		
Basement		
Attic		
Fireplace		
Spa in bath		
Air-conditioning		
Wall-to-wall carpet		
Hardwood floors		
View		
Light (windows)		
Shade		

(Copyright 2006. Reprinted with permission from REALTOR® Magazine Online.)

CHAPTER 4

Mortgage Alternatives

While it's flattering to let banks compete over you, as some companies suggest, applying for a loan is a complicated process requiring some preparation on your part. Among other considerations, you'll want to look at your credit history to see if there are any glitches you can fix before you talk to a lender. You'll need documents, including pay stubs, bank statements, tax returns, and revolving charges (monthly payments on credit cards, autos, boats, etc.).

Preapproved versus Prequalified

There are advantages and disadvantages to types of lenders, loans, and terms that you'll need to check out. Most important, you'll have to decide on a range, not an exact figure, that you can afford to spend on a home.

Before you shop for a home, you'll need to get *preapproved* by a lender, which means the lender has actually evaluated your personal finances and has agreed to give you a *preapproval letter*. A lender's preapproval means you have passed their criteria to qualify for a loan for a certain amount, but loan approval doesn't happen until you actually purchase a home and the lender can process the price of the home, a market appraisal, and underwriting for final approval. Once a loan is approved, it can close quickly.

But beware. There are plenty of online self-qualifying sites that allow you to print out a *prequalification*. That just means that according to the information you put in, you qualify for a certain loan and amount. That's not the same as a preapproval. Prequalification sites have no way of knowing if the information you put in is correct, so their preapproval doesn't mean anything. Unless the lender is evaluating real financial documents that you've provided, including pay stubs, bank statements, tax records, and credit accounts, not just information you've keyed into an automated prequalifier, it's not a true preapproval.

If you want to be treated like a real buyer—with respect—you need to be *prepared*. Your agent will want you to be preapproved by a lender before she takes you out to view homes. This is for your protection as well as hers.

When you're preapproved, you're ready to buy. If you're in a hot market where the seller is receiving multiple offers, having a preapproval letter can move your offer to the top of the heap because the seller knows you are ready to proceed to closing.

In fact, some agents won't allow you to enter their sellers' listings without a bona fide preapproval. It's their job to protect sellers from having their time wasted. A true buyer is capable of making an offer and heading toward closing; a lookie-loo is interested in anything but making an offer on the home.

Some buyer's agents won't take you out to view homes without a preapproval because they know from experience that buyers who aren't preapproved are much less likely to buy a home. One study by Campbell Communications in 2005 found that of realty agents interviewed, nearly 40 percent said buyers working with Internet lenders' preapprovals were the most likely to fail to close.

To make sure you have a preapproval that will win the respect of the most discerning seller or agent, make sure it includes the information that has been checked and evaluated, such as your credit history, employment, and other pertinent data, as well as the maximum amount at a specified interest rate you are approved for (subject to the lender's third-party appraisal of the home).

Online Calculators

You can play with an online calculator to get an idea of where you stand, and prequalify yourself on hundreds of real estate and lending sites. Many use automated mortgage calculators as lead generation tools for mortgage lenders and agents.

Online calculators tabulate easy-entry data—interest rates, gross annual income, monthly debt payments—to produce the price of a home you can afford according to conventional loan (loans that are guaranteed by the government) guidelines. Some calculate what your monthly payments would be. It's good to try several different calculators to give yourself an idea of the range you can comfortably afford.

Of course, these calculators offer the best-case scenario; they're missing the details that drive up the monthly costs of owning a home—property taxes, insurance, utilities, and other costs.

Depending on the perspective of the sites you choose, you'll usually be directed to talk to a lender before you do anything. For example, go to the Mortgage Banker's Association web site, www.mbaa.org, to the section called "Home Loan Learning Center," and you can be taken through a tutorial. Most tutorials tell you something like this:

- See a lender.
- Figure out how much you can afford.
- See loan options.
- Find a home.
- Submit loan application.

If only shopping for a loan were that simple! How do you choose a lender from the myriad of options available? A quick solution is to ask your agent. While your agent may not be a lender, he certainly works with professional lenders all the time.

Lending problems, such as not getting loan approval in time or last-minute requests for documentation, are the number one reason why home purchases fail to close. Your agent will know which lenders in the area are reliable, professional, and closing date–oriented. One day may not make a lot of difference to a lender, but it makes a huge difference to you if you're sitting in the driveway with all your belongings in the moving truck.

Professionalism and customer service are paramount. If your agent has to work in partnership with your lender for a successful, on-time closing, it is advisable to seek your agent's opinion on the performance of lenders you are considering. A lender who cannot close within the time specified in a contracted sale agreement may cost you your purchase. Most agents will have a list of lenders they find effective and who were successful with previous buyers.

You should interview several lenders before making your choice, because some lenders offer better deals than others, but that's only important to you if your lender is motivated to get you closed on time.

Mortgage Brokers or Bankers?

A *mortgage broker* is licensed by the state to sell loans to consumers. Mortgage brokers don't lend you the money directly, but they take your loan application, look it over, and decide which of the lenders in their stable of contacts are most likely to offer you a loan you'll like. Mortgage brokers aren't able to issue you a preapproval letter because they aren't loaning the money. A *mortgage banker* works directly for the institution loaning the money, and can issue you a preapproval letter personally.

Sometimes it's not clear whether you're working with a broker or banker, but you can certainly ask how the lender is being paid. A broker may be paid in the form of *points*—one point is one percent of the loan price.

The advantage to working with a mortgage broker is that they will take one application with one fee to pull your credit report. If you apply with a mortgage lender, your fee is only good at that bank. That can make a difference when you're comparing loans from savings and loans, commercial banks, mortgage companies, and credit unions.

Your Records

You'll need to get your financial records in order, including:

- W-2 forms, or business tax return forms if you're self-employed, for the last two or three years for every person signing the loan.
- Copies of one or more months of pay stubs from every person signing the loan.
- Copies of two to four months of bank or credit union statements for both checking and savings accounts, and so on.

Lenders generally require a credit report, which they will get themselves. While you've already obtained one, so you can take care of any discrepancies, lenders want to see for themselves what kind of risk you pose.

Tip: While shopping for lenders, don't let them each pull your credit report, as that could use up valuable points on your FICO score. It's the score that helps determine your interest rate. Compare loan programs first. When you're ready to choose a lender, then let that lender pull your credit. Wait to compare interest rates when you are ready to lock.

Clean Up Your Credit

You may think you know what kind of shape your credit is in, but there are companies in the United States that measure and track such things and compile all the data that is reported to them. The service they provide is not to you, but to lenders, landlords, employers, and others to minimize their risk in loaning you money, renting you housing, or giving you employment.

These three credit reporting agencies operate independently, compiling your information into a credit score, which provides a quick view of your personal credit history. Many lenders use nothing but your credit score, coupled with one or two reports, to make the decision to give you a mortgage and at what rate of interest.

Here's how it works. The three credit reporting bureaus are Equifax (www.equifax.com), Experian (www.experian.com), and TransUnion (www.transunion.com). Each receives information from a variety of sources, including credit cards, installment loans, auto loans, rental histories, and more. They post the information into a *credit file disclosure*, a report that tracks the consumer's payment record. The results reveal if the consumer pays on time, pays in full, or leaves accounts to be collected.

The Federal Trade Commission has mandated a single centralized point for consumers to find out their personal credit histories. That source is www.Annualcreditreport.com, which is operated by all three credit reporting bureaus.

Still, the credit reporting bureaus don't make it easy; each bureau requires you to submit a separate application to receive a report. Once the web site receives your request, it must deliver your complete report within 15 days. The reports will arrive separately, accompanied by a list of the consumer's federal credit rights and a toll-free number to get help or more information.

According to Annualcreditreport.com, a credit file disclosure includes all the payment information that has been collected about you, plus a record of "everyone who has received a consumer report about you from the consumer reporting company within a certain period of time ('inquiries')."

"The credit file disclosure," continues the web site, "includes certain information that is not included in a consumer report about you to a third party, such as the inquiries of companies for preapproved offers of credit or insurance and account reviews, and any medical account information which is suppressed for third party users of consumer reports."

Credit reports or disclosures include your payment history, level of debt, negative remarks, notices of liens or judgments, types of credit and use, the level of monthly payments, number of credit cards, how much credit is used versus unused, credit inquiries, and other information.

All of this information is collected for credit scoring. A *credit score* is a "complex mathematical model that evaluates many types of information in a credit file," says Annualcreditreport.com. "A credit score is used by a lender to help determine whether a person qualifies for a particular credit card, loan, or service. Most credit scores estimate the *risk* a company incurs by lending a person money or providing them with a service—specifically, the likelihood that the person will make payments on time in the next two to three years."

Scores range from 200 to 850. The lowest scores indicate a consumer is a poor credit risk. Low scores will mean fewer approvals for credit and higher interest rates. High scores indicate consumers are more creditworthy, smoothing the way for easy loan approval, wider choices of loan packages, and cheaper interest rates.

At publication time, a free peek at credit reports is available, but unfortunately this does not include credit scores. However, you can access your scores by paying a reasonable fee. To make matters more confusing, there isn't just one credit score to be found. Fair Isaac, the first company to provide credit scoring under its "FICO" brand, is only one of several. You can find your FICO scores at www.myfico.com.

Credit bureaus can spell trouble for you, because the information they have may not be accurate or up to date, or may not even relate to your credit record but to someone else's. Worse, they operate independently. One bureau may have correct information,

Five Factors That Decide Your Credit Score

Credit scores range between 200 and 850. Scores above 620 are considered desirable for obtaining a mortgage. These factors will affect your score.

1. *Your payment history*—whether you paid credit card obligations on time.

2. *How much you owe.* Owing a great deal of money on numerous accounts can indicate that you are overextended.

3. *The length of your credit history*—in general, the longer the better.

4. *How much new credit you have.* New credit, either installment payments or new credit cards, is considered more risky, even if you pay promptly.

5. *The types of credit you use.* Generally, it's desirable to have more than one type of credit—installment loans, credit cards, and a mortgage, for example.

For more on evaluating and understanding your credit score, go to www.myfico.com.

(Copyright 2006. Reprinted with permission from REALTOR® Magazine Online.)

while another may have erroneous information. That leaves it up to the consumer to check all three credit bureaus for errors. In addition, you have separate credit scores from each bureau. One may score you more highly than another, because each uses its own statistical models as well as the information it has, which may or may not be accurate.

According to troubling information compiled in 2004 and 2005 by Opinion Research for the Consumer Federation of America (CFA) and Providian Financial, most borrowers don't understand how seriously credit scores can affect them. Many don't know that the lower their score the less chance they have of obtaining a mortgage with a low interest rate. Two-thirds of consumers surveyed didn't understand that maxing out their credit cards influences their scores, and many didn't understand that credit card companies as well as mortgage lenders base the interest rates they charge on credit scores.

The good news is that over 90 percent of consumers understood that late payments and nonpayment would impact their credit scores, but most didn't understand that insurers, cell phone companies, and numerous other service providers make their decisions to provide service based on credit scores.

One of the largest real estate franchising companies in the nation, GMAC, also had a survey conducted by Caravan Opinion Research Corp., which found similar results, says Broderick Perkins, contributor to *Realty Times*.

"Most consumers, 62 percent, did not know that a score above 620 out of 850 is necessary to secure the most favorable mortgage rate," says Perkins. "More than 50 percent incorrectly answered that increased income level will raise one's credit score. A boat load of disposable income doesn't amount to a hill of beans when it comes to your credit score if you have a high debt-to-income ratio, maxed-out credit cards, or even numerous credit cards with small balances and high credit limits."

GMAC found that only 42 percent of consumers knew that payment history was a critical determinant to a credit score, says Perkins. "If you tend to miss payments your score will suffer. If you are on time, all the time, your score will improve."

Dos and Don'ts

The most important step you can take toward buying a home is to get your credit in order. Too few consumers check their credit in time to purchase, and end up with higher interest rates because they didn't know there was a problem until the lender discovered it.

The Dos of Managing Your Credit

Check Your Credit Disclosure and Scores at Annualcredit report.com or Myfico.com.   Do this before you talk to a lender, at least one month in advance if possible. That will give you time to correct inaccurate information with the credit reporting bureau(s). Credit problems that have to be resolved take time and may impact both how soon you can close on a loan and how much the loan will cost you. That's why it's smart to clean up your credit before you talk to a lender.

Use Alternative Credit Reports and Scores to Boost Your Scores. New alternative credit reports and scores based on on-time payments to landlords, utilities, cable companies, and other accounts that aren't included in the three primary credit bureau files are available through the National Credit Reporting Association and

PRBC, a national credit bureau that reports nontraditional credit information.

Improve Your Credit Now.   It's never too late to start making payments on time, controlling your debt, and saving some cash, but don't expect your credit scores to improve overnight. Start sending in payments early, so you don't get hit with "overdue" notices that result in late fees.

Make Sure Your Credit Issues Were Caused by You and Not Someone Else.   You may have to supply copies of divorce decrees, loan applications, and other documentation to show that an account you are being cited as delinquent for is not really yours. Remove authorized users such as teenagers if they are causing delinquencies that are pulling your credit scores down.

Build Credit with a Few Necessities.   You'll need four to six months to build a record, but if you want to establish credit, start with a secure credit card account, a gasoline card, and a small personal loan. These are called unsecured loans. Expect to pay higher interest for an unsecured loan than a loan secured by property such as a house or car. Pay your balances on time. If you have never opened an account, establishing credit is something that will take time because what the lenders look at is your payment history—not the fact that you don't have any debt. Establish good credit by repaying the loans promptly.

Don'ts of Managing Your Credit

Don't Take on New Debt.   Don't open new accounts or make major purchases. To buy the most home you can, you'll need as much cash and credit as you can get. Talk to your agent and lender about which strategies are best for your situation, whether it's making minimum payments and using cash for a down payment, or paying off debt and rolling the down payment into your mortgage.

Avoid Credit Repair Companies. Negative entries on your credit report, if true, can't be erased. Credit repair companies work by sending letters to credit bureaus that dispute the negative items. Under the law, the credit bureau must respond within 30 days or remove the disputed item from its record. The problem is that the creditor will refile the item so your disputed item doesn't disappear for long, and can come back just in time to kill your loan.

The Federal Trade Commission (www.ftc.gov) advises that credit repair clinics "don't do anything for consumers that consumers cannot do for themselves at little or no cost. Beware of any organization that offers to create a new identity and credit file for you."

Here are some warning signs that the FTC and others say consumers should look out for:

- An organization that guarantees to remove late payments, bankruptcies, or similar information from a credit report.
- An organization that charges a lot of money to repair credit.
- A company that asks the consumer to write to the credit reporting company and repeatedly seek verification of the

same credit account information in the file, month after month, even though the information has been determined to be correct.

- An organization that is reluctant to give out its address or one that pushes you to make a decision immediately.

Rather than risk wasting time and money, contact consumer credit companies that can advise you, such as the Consumer Credit Counseling Service (www.cccsintl.org) or the Institute of Consumer Financial Education (www.financial-education-icfe.org).

Don't Pay Collection Agencies.   Pay the creditor directly. While you can't expect a derogatory entry to be removed from your report, paying it off can't hurt with your creditor. Don't be afraid to ask a favor. Tell the creditor you are buying a house and would like them to remove the fact that your payments were late. Some will, some won't. Be sure to obtain a letter saying that the balance is paid in full. Keep in mind that while one bureau may show the account as paid, you may have to prove it to the other.

Don't Close Long-Established Credit Accounts with Good Payment Histories.   Closing accounts with long-established credit histories eliminates examples of your good payment history, which is what lenders are looking for.

If you want to understand how important your FICO score is to the interest rate you'll be charged, consider this: If you have a FICO score below 639 and seek a 30-year fixed rate mortgage of $216,000, you'll pay $151 more per month in higher interest rates than someone with a score of 760 would pay.

**Interest Rates and Monthly Payments
for $216,000 30-Year Fixed Rate Mortgage**

FICO Score	Interest Rate	Monthly Payment
760–850	6.29%	$1,335
700–759	6.51%	$1,367
680–699	6.69%	$1,392
660–679	6.90%	$1,423
640–659	7.33%	$1,486
620–639	7.88%	$1,567

Source: MyFico.Com.

Types of Loans

There are so many types of loans available today that they could fill a book.

The costs of your loan(s) depend on several factors—your credit history, how much money you are putting down, and your income-to-debt ratio, as well as how much home you are trying to buy.

Begin with the rates that are available. Generally speaking, the more favorable the terms are to the borrower, the higher risk to the borrower.

The benchmark of housing loans is the *30-year fixed rate*. When you see mortgage rates quoted online or on TV, this is the standard. A *fixed rate* means that the terms and costs of the loan are fixed for the term of the loan. Even if interest rates escalate dramatically, your loan's interest is fixed at that rate. Other costs may go up—your property taxes and insurance—but the cost of your loan will stay the same for the term of the loan. Fixed rate mortgage loans are available for any term, but the 30-year, 20-year, 15-year, 10-year, and 5-year terms are the most popular.

The benefits of a fixed rate mortgage are that consumers have no surprises, and the loan rate never changes unless you sell or refinance. The disadvantage of a fixed rate mortgage is that you may pay a higher interest rate than necessary if you sell your home in four or five years or less, which can be like buying more insurance than you may actually need.

An *adjustable rate* means the interest rate of the loan may adjust to rate environments, causing the cost of your loan to fluctuate up or down. The loan product you choose determines how often your loan adjusts (usually once a year) and at what increments (for example, no more than 2 percent higher than the previous annual adjustment with a 5 percent cap). The benefit of adjustable rate mortgages is that they are much less expensive than fixed rate mortgages. Your rate can go down, saving you money that you can put toward your principal. The disadvantage of adjustable rate mortgages is that they are especially risky in an inflationary environment when interest rates are headed up.

Hybrid, balloon, or convertible loans combine the most favorable features of both fixed and adjustable rate loans, and are an ideal compromise for borrowers who aren't sure how long they will be in their homes. The hybrid combines fixed rates for a period of 1 to

10 years, and then the loan rolls over to an adjustable period for the remaining term of the loan. Balloon loans are even less expensive, but they come due at the end of a five- or seven-year term. The advantage of this type of loan is that you can choose the term of the fixed rate segment of your loan for the period of time you think you'll most likely stay in your home. The disadvantage is that with a period of years between adjustments, markets can change radically, with much higher interest rates to come after your fixed period ends.

Interest-only loans are loaned for repayment of interest only; the lender does not use any of the borrower's monthly payment to pay down the principal (the borrowed amount). These loans are much cheaper to borrowers than loans that pay principal, allowing them to buy more house with less money, but they are also riskier, and borrowers must rely on an appreciating market to build equity. Interest-only loans are also available as hybrid loans, coupled with adjustable rate loans. The advantage to interest-only loans is that they are among the cheapest loans since no money is applied toward paying down principal. The disadvantage is that if markets don't deliver anticipated appreciation gains, borrowers could find themselves owing more than the home's market value.

Zero-down loans don't require a down payment, but you'll pay a higher interest rate as well as a higher mortgage insurance multiplier. (Private mortgage insurance is required by some lenders to offset the risks of loaning the full value of the home.) This is an option if you want to buy but saving for a down payment is a long way off, or if you intend to get into a home and stay there while taking advantage of an already low interest rate. The advantage of a zero-down loan is that you get to leverage more of your lender's money while writing off the interest on your income taxes. The disadvantage is that you have less equity in the home.

Seller Financing

Because of the ready availability of mortgages requiring little or no down payment and easier money for borrowers with less than perfect credit (subprime loans), sellers aren't as likely to offer to assist buyers with financing the purchase of their homes. But there are situations in which it may be helpful.

A seller may ask more for the property in exchange for letting you buy it on contract. The advantage to the seller is that they have mailbox money while you make your payments. However, if you default, the seller still owns the property.

When a seller finances your mortgage, they serve as your lender. With a traditional mortgage, the lender owns the promissory note on the property until you pay the mortgage back. With seller financing, the seller owns the promissory note until you pay the mortgage back. The advantage to you is that you have a promissory note that you must pay back, just like any mortgage, but you have saved thousands in lender fees, as well as a down payment, PMI insurance, and other costs.

You can get the transaction done at a title company or attorney's office, but make sure that the seller owns the property free and clear. If the seller does not own the property free and clear and another owner or lien-holder claims the property, you will most likely lose your money.

There are numerous types of loans that may fit your situation. Your lender will help advise you as to the right type of loan for your needs, but remember that a lot of the loans available today are a reflection of rising house values, and may be higher risk or higher cost than you want. Among them are negative amortization ("neg-am") loans in which borrowers have a choice to pay principal and interest or just interest. When they don't pay principal for a given payment, that amount is added to the back end of the note, which means that borrowers can end up owing more on the home than its purchase price. Another higher-risk loan is the 40-year fixed rate, which is popular in high-flying markets such as California and Florida which have experienced double-digit percent home price increases over the last five years. Specialty loans are designed to get people into homes more affordably, but they also get people in who simply want to buy a more expensive home *now*.

NAR advises caution when choosing a loan. While it's tempting to be able to leverage the lender to buy more house than you ever dreamed you could afford, you also must calculate the risks.

Home buyers may not realize that monthly payments on some types of specialty mortgages can increase by as much as 50 percent or more when the introductory period ends. For that reason, NAR and the Center for Responsible Lending have partnered to create a new brochure for home buyers, specifically addressing specialty loans and abusive lending practices, called "Specialty Mortgages: What Are the Risks and Advantages?" You can ask your agent for a copy of the brochure or access it online on NAR's consumer web site at www.realtor.org/housing opportunity. The brochure is also available through the Center for Responsible Lending at www.responsiblelending.org.

Most home buyers stay in their homes a little over five years. First-time home buyers move more quickly to another home, while repeat buyers tend to stay in their next home longer, perhaps because of school-age children, job stability, and other reasons.

While it's impossible to see into the future, you should think carefully about what you are most likely to do. Are you likely to add to your family and need a bigger place? Are you likely to seek transfers? Those answers can help you pick the right loan.

Annual Percentage Rates

Getting the mortgage interest rate is only the first step. The second is finding out what the true cost of the loan will be. The annual percentage rate combines the mortgage interest rate with other loan package fees that have been rolled into the note, such as *points* (percentages paid to the lender or the broker as commissions; paying more points results in a lower interest rate) or other fees to cover costs such as title work, appraisals, underwriting fees, settlement costs, and other processing fees.

Some of these fees are negotiable, while others aren't. When you are comparing loans side by side, do the following:

- Compare interest rates among lenders at the same time on the same day.
- Ask for written estimates of fees.
- Ask for better terms if you can see that certain fees are negotiable.

Locking In Your Rate

Once you have negotiated with your favorite lenders, pick the one you think you can work with the best and lock in your rate. In a market where interest rates are fluctuating, having a locked-in rate can protect you if the markets get rattled. Your locked rate agreement should include the interest rate, the period of the lock-up (usually 60 days), and the number of points (percentage points) to be paid. If you ask for a lock, expect to pay an appraisal fee up front.

If rates should fall, you can do one of two things: Negotiate lower terms with your lender or initiate a new loan with your number two choice. The trick is getting the loan to close in time so you can take possession of your house. If a lender feels that you won't have time to get a lower rate and close, he may hold firm to the locked-in rate, because that loan is already in motion and partway through underwriting (the phase where the insurer looks at the loan and decides if it is a good risk).

This is not a game of chicken for the fainthearted. You could seriously jeopardize your closing by changing lenders at the last minute. To be on the safe side, try to negotiate a locked rate with one float down so that if rates go lower, you'll at least get the next lowest rate. But be prepared, once again, to pay the lender on the back end for this service.

When your lender processes your loan application, you will receive a *good faith estimate* within three days. The estimate outlines your closing costs, which will include all your application fees, title costs, attorney's fees, surveys, appraisals, document preparation fees, recording fees, and more. You may pay some fees up front such as credit report fees and appraisals, depending on the lender.

If You Have Damaged Credit

Don't assume that if you have less-than-perfect credit you won't be able to buy a home. There are all kinds of lenders with all kinds of loan products that are happy to serve you. If you have damaged credit, or wish to buy a home that doesn't meet conforming loan limits, simply be prepared to pay a higher interest rate.

Conventional lenders can help you whether you have late payments, judgments, tax liens, or bankruptcies. You'll be put into a *subprime* loan, which means you aren't a prime credit risk, but that doesn't mean you will pay so much more in interest that you'll never be able to repay the loan. Any lender is interested in seeing you pay off your loan, and you may even find that compared to some conventional loan programs, you're only paying slightly more. Subprime loans are graded according to risk, so a person who has lost a job, had some late payments, but is back on track won't pay the same rate as someone with years of credit abuse on their record.

Your lender will work with you to get you the best rate possible, and may have a product for you that will actually help you repair your credit if you make your payments on time and in full.

Special Programs for First-Time Home Buyers, Veterans, and Workforce Personnel

The Department of Housing and Urban Development (HUD) is a tremendous resource for first-time home buyers, displaced home-makers, single parents, and workforce personnel such as teachers, police, and firefighters. Several agencies under the HUD umbrella help consumers buy homes.

The Federal Housing Administration (FHA), for example, supplies home mortgages that are sold through lenders. The FHA doesn't make loans to the public—it insures the loans so lenders are more willing to make them. These are the lowest-cost loans available because borrowers conform to certain criteria. Among these criteria is the ratio of loan debt to income.

In order to prevent home buyers from getting into a home they cannot afford, debt-to-income ratios are used to calculate whether the potential borrower is in a financial position that would allow them to meet the demands that are often included in owning a home, according to the FHA web site (www.FHA.com).

Two types of ratios are considered: mortgage debt to income, and total debt to income.

Mortgage Debt to Income

To calculate the ratio of mortgage debt to income, add up the total mortgage payment (principal, or the amount to be borrowed, plus interest, escrow deposits for taxes, hazard insurance, mortgage insurance premium, homeowners' dues, etc.). Then divide that amount by the gross monthly income. The maximum ratio to qualify is 28 percent.

Here's an example:

Total amount of new house payment	$ 750
Borrower's gross monthly income	$2,850
Divide total house payment by gross income	$\dfrac{750}{2,850}$
Debt-to-income ratio	26.32%

Total Debt to Income

To get this amount, add up the total mortgage payment (principal and interest, escrow deposits for taxes, hazard insurance, mortgage insurance premium, homeowners' dues, etc.) and all recurring monthly revolving and installment debt (car loans, personal loans, student loans, credit cards, etc.). Then divide that amount by the gross monthly income. The maximum ratio to qualify is 41 percent.

Look at this example:

Total amount of new house payment	$ 750
Total amount of monthly recurring debt	$ 400
Total amount of monthly debt	$1,150
Borrower's gross monthly income (including spouse, if married)	$2,850
Divide total monthly debt by gross monthly income	$\dfrac{1,150}{2,850}$
Debt-to-income ratio	40.35%

Most conventional loans require total debt to be no more than 36 percent of income.

Good Neighbor Next Door Program

With workforce housing becoming more unaffordable every day, the Department of Housing and Urban Development (HUD) has created special borrowing programs for teachers, police, and fire-fighters. The programs allow these backbones of community life to buy HUD housing at a significant discount in "revitalization" areas. These are defined as "HUD-designated neighborhoods in need of economic and community development and where there is already a strong commitment by the local governments" (www.hud.gov/goodneighbor). Participants must be employed full-time, be able to certify their employment, and commit to living in their new residence for three years after purchase, and they cannot own any other home when they close on their HUD home.

The Teacher Next Door program is open to any person "employed full-time by a public school, private school, or federal, state, county, or municipal educational agency as a state-certified classroom teacher or administrator in grades K-12." Participants must be in good standing and certify that they are employed by an educational agency that serves the school district/jurisdiction in which the home they are purchasing is located.

The Officer Next Door program is designed to bring safety to revitalization areas. It's open to any full-time, sworn law enforcement officer who is "employed full-time by a federal, state, county, or municipal government; or a public or private college or university." They must be "sworn to uphold, and make arrests for violations of, federal, state, county, or municipal law." Their employer must certify that they are a full-time police officer with the general power of arrest.

The Firefighter Next Door program is open to full-time firefighter or emergency medical technicians employed "by a fire department or emergency medical services responder unit of the federal government, a state, a unit of general local government, or an Indian tribal government serving the area where the home is located." The employer must certify that the applicant is a full-time firefighter or emergency medical technician as described here. The applicant must meet this employment requirement "both at the time the firefighter or emergency medical technician submits a bid to purchase the home, and at the time of closing on the purchase of the home."

To learn more, go to www.hud.gov/goodneighbor.

Reverse Mortgage Programs

The FHA also assists older homeowners to stay in their homes. Through its Home Equity Conversion Mortgage (HECM), FHA helps homeowners who are over 62 years of age remain in their homes by allowing them to access their home's equity. They can use the extra income to meet monthly expenses while remaining in the homes they love.

Cash Back

At www.FHA.com you can find a network of participating real estate agents who offer cash back up to $1,000 to home buyers and sellers in most states. To qualify, you must obtain a preapproval from the FHA.com mortgage center. The money comes from the participating real estate agents as incentives to help first-time and low-income home buyers.

Down payment assistance programs are available at the local housing authority level, and generally require that the borrower's income meets guidelines for assistance. To learn more, visit www.fha.com, and look for FHA Down Payment Grants.

VA Programs

Included in the GI Bill is a benefit to America's veterans that allows them to purchase homes without making a down payment. They can use the VA Fixed Rate Loan and finance their mortgages over 15-, 20-, 25-, or 30-year terms with the interest rate remaining fixed for the life of the loan.

According to the FHA web site, VA loans are guaranteed by the Department of Veterans Affairs and can be used to "purchase a single family home, including a townhouse or condominium unit in a VA approved project, to build a home, and purchase and improve a home. Loans are assumable under certain conditions and do not have a prepayment penalty."

VA financing is available to veterans of the armed services, those currently in active duty or the reserves, and their spouses. In order to qualify for a VA loan veterans must be eligible as defined by the Department of Veterans Affairs. Veterans can qualify to put zero down on a loan up to $417,000. VA Fixed Rate Loans are full documentation loans, which means the veteran must provide full financial disclosure. Before closing, a funding fee must be collected from the borrower and can be financed into the loan. Funding fee exemption is possible upon proper verification of disability, says the site.

Veterans who are eligible can also qualify for the Interest Rate Reduction Refinance program, which involves transferring one VA mortgage loan to another loan. The terms of the refinance are similar to those of other loans, carrying with it 15-, 20-, 25-, or 30-year options on fixed rate mortgages. Loans are assumable under certain conditions without a prepayment penalty.

Local Housing Authorities

Cities have local housing authorities that administer bond programs that help first-time home buyers and in-fill buyers. To find these programs, visit HUD's "Home buying programs in your state" at www.hud.gov/local buying. Find your state, then scroll down to your city and click. You'll be taken to your local city or town Housing Authority, or city housing department.

For example, Dallas offers mortgage assistance programs for first-time home buyers that provide principal reduction, down payment assistance, and closing costs up to $12,000. The housing department can also provide a grant up to $1,500 for repairs. To qualify, home buyers must receive home ownership education from an approved counseling agency, buy a home in Dallas, and the sales price of the home cannot exceed federal loan limits.

First-time home buyers include more people than newbies who have never bought a home before. Under many first-time home buyer programs, single parents and displaced homemakers are automatically considered. That's a break for many people, because HUD programs, which are generally qualified for at the local housing level, provide special access to HUD housing and special interest rates on loans.

The local housing authority will also have lists of other home buyer incentives, such as tax abatements to purchase in certain areas. In many cities, property buyers are getting special breaks on their property taxes in order to revitalize designated urban areas.

Private Sector Assistance Programs for Home Buyers

In addition, there are nonprofit programs to assist borrowers, some of which are based on the buyer being able to qualify for a loan that allows down payment assistance gifts, such as those provided through the Nehemiah Corporation (www.nehemiahcorp.org) or Ameridream (www.ameridream.org).

To qualify, home buyers must purchase within conforming loan limits up to $359,650. What these programs typically do is provide a down payment "gift" to the lender on behalf of the seller, which means that the house will sell for slightly more in order to cover the "gift." The advantage to the borrower is that they don't have to come up with as much cash. The disadvantage is that they pay more for the house, but they are getting into a home they might not have had the cash to buy otherwise.

Assistance programs are a trade-off. If it's worth it to you to buy in a revitalized neighborhood, help a city get back on its feet, and pay a little more to get into a home, these programs are the best way to meet that goal.

Seller Assist

If you find the house you want, and want it for a little less, instead of asking for a reduction in sales price, find out if the seller is willing to meet you halfway with closing costs.

Sellers may not advertise that they'd be willing to help you with closing costs, because savvy sellers will reserve their wiggle room for a true negotiation with an eminent buyer. So don't assume that any ad you see is written in stone.

Realty Times columnist M. Anthony Carr suggests reading the fine print, looking for phrases like "decorating allowance," or "Seller to assist buyer up to 3 percent." These items are "seller subsidies."

"Even in the long haul, sometimes the $5,000 subsidy means more to the buyer than a $10,000 price reduction and it may be more beneficial to you as a buyer to go for larger subsidies instead of a price reduction," advises Carr. "The ultimate win for a buyer would be to get both."

Sellers may be more willing to subsidize buyers in certain markets like buyer's markets (when housing sales go soft and buyers have more negotiating power) or in slow sales months such as wintertime. Sometimes sellers can shoot themselves in the foot by overpricing, allowing their homes to stagnate on the market. They are more likely to negotiate a seller subsidy over a price reduction.

Ten Questions to Ask Your Lender

Be sure you find a loan that fits your needs with these comprehensive questions.

1. What are the most popular mortgage loans you offer?

2. Which type of mortgage plan do you think would be best for us? Why?

3. Are your rates, terms, fees, and closing costs negotiable?

4. Will I have to buy private mortgage insurance? If so how much will it cost and how long will it be required? *Note:* Private mortgage insurance usually is required if you make less than a 20 percent down payment, but most lenders will let you discontinue the policy when you've acquired a certain amount of equity by paying down the loan.

5. Who will service the loan? Your bank or another company?

6. What escrow requirements do you have?

7. How long is your loan lock-in period (the time that the quoted interest rate will be honored)? Will I be able to obtain a lower rate if they drop during this period?

8. How long will the loan approval process take?

9. How long will it take to close the loan?

10. Are there any charges or penalties for prepaying the loan?

Used with permission from Real Estate Checklists & Systems (http://www.realestatechecklists.com).

(Copyright 2006. Reprinted with permission from REALTOR® Magazine Online.)

Lenders limit seller subsidies because they would ideally like to see the buyer put more money into the house, assuring they'll be less likely to default on a loan.

"Keep in mind, how you word the cash that's being left at the table determines whether or not it is a seller subsidy," explains Carr. "If, for instance, after the home inspection, it's determined the house needs a new roof and the seller agrees to fix it, this is generally not called a 'subsidy.' The seller is just agreeing to bring the house up to par. However, if the buyer requests $10,000 for a decorating allowance and then spends it on the roof, they have just negotiated a subsidy from the seller." The wording and agreement in exchange of money is important in order to meet state laws governing the transfer of real estate.

When shopping for your mortgage, remember that you are choosing your lender as well, so be prepared to ask everything you need to know to help you make the best decision. Use the "Ten Questions to Ask Your Lender" list (see page 101) to be sure you find a loan that fits your needs.

CHAPTER 5

Types of Homes— Which Fits Your Needs Best?

There are plenty of ways to situate yourself and your family—economically, socially, culturally, and geographically. If you have a family with children, you can buy a home in a neighborhood known for its emphasis on schools and recreational opportunities, so your kids can grow up with playmates, teammates, and lots of activities. Or, if you're in an adult household, you may prefer a more urban lifestyle that is more focused on activities and interests for singles, couples, and nontraditional families of all ages. In other words, do you want to be closer to playgrounds or nightlife? Or both?

Single-family homes are still regarded as the gold standard of real estate in most areas, but changing demographics suggest that there may be wonderful lifestyle opportunities in condominiums, townhomes, and high-rises. It all depends on what you want for yourself, your partner or roommate, or your family.

Forty-nine percent of the home-buying public are married with children under the age of 18 living at home, according to NAR. Single-family homes are great for many people, but a good many home buyers are finding they like multifamily living. In the past few years, condominiums have made an incredible comeback, outpacing family homes in terms of appreciation and popularity with buyers. And it's not because of cheaper prices—in 2005 and 2006 the median value of condos was higher than the median value of homes. In early 2006, NAR found that the national median existing condo price was $214,300, while the median single-family home price was $209,000.

Neighborhoods are either on their way up to higher prices because of new construction, local amenities, and schools, or they are on their way down due to aging homes and facilities that aren't being as well maintained. Then one day a developer, builder, or other entrepreneur decides to take advantage of depreciating values and reinvent the area, possibly with new products such as apartments, townhomes, or senior communities.

Demographics change and so do personal preferences. In the 1950s, you could not have given away a home with an open kitchen, yet today, that's what home buyers want. They want transparency and to feel connected with other occupants, because today's buyer works long, hard hours and time with family is precious.

Affordability, density, and other market conditions also impact the types of homes available. When home prices or utility costs become an issue, homes with smaller square footage suddenly become more attractive.

Fixer-uppers have also become more popular with buyers. A run-down home in a middling neighborhood near public transportation could be the next hot makeover bargain.

What are your preferences? Do you like antiques, collectibles, and vintage architecture, or are you fond of chrome, glass, and no clutter? Believe it or not, your tastes may change as you live with one style and evolve into another style.

The U.S. Census says that young single home buyers are the fastest-growing segment. The number of homeowners younger than 25 has doubled over the last 10 years to 1.64 million from 807,000, but they aren't all moving to suburbia. That's not so surprising when you consider the relaxed lending standards of today. The opportunity is available for young people to invest in housing who were shut out or delayed a generation ago when lenders stuck closely to the 20 percent down rule. And they are bringing their generation's outlook on home and design with them—an eclectic, colorful tweaking of old versus new.

What you're seeing when you see a neighborhood start to boom is other people recognizing opportunity. If you want to look at home buying as an investment, then you have to be the pioneer, the one who recognizes a bargain before others do. Other home buyers will watch what you do, and when they see that you've stuck your proverbial toe in the water, and it's fine, they may join you in rehabbing an older neighborhood and turning it into the hottest enclave in the city.

What people pay for when they buy a home is largely risk mitigation. When they pay more, they are assuming there will be less risk in selling the home because of its desirability. If they pay less, they are more likely to embrace the fact that their neighborhood and house aren't as in demand by the market.

Anyway, you won't be stuck for long. People are migratory by nature. They will always be looking for the next good thing—the bigger home, the better studio apartment, the high-rise with the best spa. Most people will move in and out of as many as four or more homes in a lifetime (every 7 to 10 years, for most homeowners).

Home Buyer Preferences

Just as cars and SUVs are downsizing a little, so are homes, which reduces the pressure on home buyers to buy more than they need. The 2,330-square-foot home is giving way to the smaller but feature-rich garden home, townhome, or condominium. Many home buyers are able to afford more than one property; they can purchase a second home as a vacation home or as an investment. But if you're buying one home, you want it to be as flexible to your needs and as affordable as possible.

Other features favored by today's homeowner are indoor and outdoor livability, innovation, and the kitchen as the hub of the house, says *Realty Times* columnist Michele Dawson in a February 15, 2005, article.

Better Homes and Gardens editors conducted a survey in February 2005, which according to Dawson offered the following conclusions:

- Approximately 68 percent of those who took the survey said they want a home that incorporates a "work from home" feature, with many planning on adopting such a lifestyle within the next five years.

- Families are staying in a home three to five years; they're moving up as their family grows. That means the homes aren't accommodating budding families.

- Approximately 69 percent completed a major remodeling project at some point over the past five years, and 42 percent plan to do so in the next five years. Both figures reflect that Americans are constantly changing their homes, says Dawson.

Flexibility is important because circumstances change. You may start working from home and suddenly find yourself needing a home office. While you can make do with the dining room table, having flexible space allows you to change the purpose of rooms to suit your needs. That means you'll need lots of storage, too, as you put away furniture and accessories you're not using while you reinvent your bonus room as a nursery, media room, or office.

National Association of Home Builders (NAHB) spokesperson Gopal Ahluwalia says that over the next five years he expects to see more demand for low-maintenance natural materials, synthetic stucco, energy efficiency, and security on the outside of the home. Inside, open space, quality features, technology, and special purpose rooms are on the upswing.

He also says the top five amenities home buyers want in their new home are a walk-in pantry, an island work area, special use storage, a built-in microwave, and drinking water filtration.

Here are some other observations from the NAHB:

- Some 37 percent of the respondents want their kitchens visually open to the family room with a half wall; 34 percent want it completely open.
- In the bathroom, home buyers want a linen closet, exhaust fan, a separate shower enclosure, and a whirlpool tub.
- Younger buyers want the washer and dryer near the bedroom; older buyers prefer the appliances near the kitchen.
- Home owners participating in focus groups complained that builders aren't putting lights in the bedroom.
- Asked to choose between more space in the master bedroom and less in the master bath, or the opposite, 69 percent chose more bedroom space. "Some of the master baths have been getting bigger than the bedrooms themselves," Ahluwalia said.
- Sixty-three percent said that they would not be willing to buy a home without a living room, but Ahluwalia predicted that living rooms will vanish from the average America house in the next five years or so.

Better Homes and Gardens suggests that a home's indoor and outdoor livability "will play a more significant role in homes of the future than ever before. Outside areas are becoming extensions of the American home's indoor living spaces, with patios, barbecue centers, decks, and other areas essentially serving as 'additional rooms.' "

Types of Housing

Just as your agent is a market specialist, she can also be an expert in types of housing, from attached housing, such as duplexes and condominiums, to single-family homes, and from new builder homes to historical homes.

For example, to buy a condominium means that you must understand the community rules and regulations and must agree to adhere to strict modification standards. An agent who is a condo specialist will know what documents to ask of the homeowners association. A new home specialist will know how to negotiate with a builder, and will alert you to ways builders boost their prices through upgrades, as well as which upgrades will net you more at resale. A historical home specialist is plugged into the local public improvement district, well versed in national and local modification regulations, and probably knows the best preservationist architects, interior designers, and contractors.

As the 30-year fixed rate mortgage is the standard in lending, the star of residential housing is the *single-family* home because it combines the ownership of land with a structure. *Single-family* means there are no shared walls, and the home is situated on a lot with a yard surrounding the home. However, single-family homes are not necessarily the most expensive or even the most desirable homes in a marketplace. That depends on other factors such as neighborhood, condition, local attractions, and buyer demand.

Single-family homes have more maintenance challenges—lawns to mow, flower beds to plant and weed, and appliances to keep repaired—but owners feel the additional effort is well worth it for the privacy, space, and personalization opportunities they afford.

Multifamily homes share walls, even if there is a firewall between the Sheetrock panels. The housing structure is built in units for rental or purchase. Examples of multifamily homes include:

- *Townhomes or row houses.* These homes are street-entry homes that are bought like single-family homes. Owners may or may not belong to a homeowners association that oversees community painting, fence repair, landscape maintenance, and so on.
- *Condominiums.* Condominium or apartment owners own the air space (square footage) of their unit, which is calculated into the total square footage and value of the total property.
- *Co-ops.* You're basically buying a piece of the association's ownership of the total property, so that you own part of the common areas as well as part of the building.

Multifamily housing appeals most to smaller families, and to those who want to avoid maintenance chores such as exterior painting, gutter cleaning, and landscaping. The homeowners association or building maintenance department charges a monthly fee to take care of these time-consuming tasks for the homeowners. The downside is that neighbors may have some right to direct the overall look and costs of running the building.

Shopping Online—The Best Places to Preview Homes

Nearly 3 out of 4 home buyers shop for homes online, and nearly 9 out of 10 seek some kind of information about home buying online. But what every home buyer wants to see are homes for sale.

Thanks to the robust, interactive nature of the Internet, you can see inside and outside homes for sale in extraordinary detail through multiple, quick-loading photos, virtual tours, and videos. Detailed information on schools, neighborhoods, and other features is only a click away.

Without question, the site with the greatest inventory of listings for sale is www.REALTOR.com. The official web site of the NATIONAL ASSOCIATION OF REALTORS®, REALTOR.com offers over 2.5 million listings for sale, more than any other single site online. Through its relationship with NAR, REALTOR.com has access to the data from nearly 900 multiple listing services across the country. Consumers can view listings quickly and easily, without registration, by keying in a zip code or city, state, and price range.

Searches can drill down to specifics such as number of bedrooms desired, number of baths, parking for cars, water views, and just about any other home buyer preference you can think of. To narrow your search, merely narrow your price range. You can ask the site to display homes with virtual tours or photos first, giving participating listing agents a chance to strut their marketing stuff.

You can also select surrounding areas to see what else might be available.

What makes the Internet great is that it's the only advertising medium where consumers and vendors can communicate directly from the ad. When you visit a web site and find a home you would like to know more about, you can click on the listing agent's contact link and ask them a question, while never leaving the web site. That's far easier than making a phone call with a newspaper in your lap and having to ask dozens of questions to find out if this is the home for you.

On the Internet, you can locate homes by zip code, price range, and features, and explore individual homes with video tours, multiple photographs, and feature finders. You can explore the neighborhood with aerial mapping, crime statistics, school information, and other data at your fingertips. You can compare your home's price to other homes that are being marketed in the area, all before you even talk to an agent.

But beware. Going online to sort through homes without your agent at your side isn't as easy as it sounds, for two reasons:

1. There is no single online location that has all the listings available in a given area.

2. Service providers, including some public web sites operated by MLSs, can give you automated results, such as sorting by zip code, type of home, or price, but even those may lack the drill-down results you want. If a home's price has been reduced, how long does the reduction take to find

its way online? In other words, are you seeing the freshest information available about all relevant listings? Also, is the home already under contract? Online providers generally do not have access to these types of details.

FSBOs

About 13 percent of previously owned homes for sale are for-sale-by-owner (FSBO, pronounced "fizz-bo"), and these homes aren't typically included in the MLS. The reason is simple: The owner is selling the home himself and isn't paying an agent for marketing it. The owner believes that you'll find the home on your own. Sites such as Craigslist.com, forsalebyowner.com, and owners.com may have for-sale-by-owner listings, but you may not find information on the particular house you are interested in. We discuss FSBOs further in Chapter 10.

Homeowners can decide how their homes are marketed to the public. You'll see a wide variance in the presentations of listings for this reason. You may know of some homes that aren't online simply because the owners don't want virtual strangers peering into their home. Some owners are willing to pay for extensive marketing that includes video that can be shown online, and some aren't.

Search Engines and Lead Generation Sites

As the most compelling communications system and advertising medium ever invented, the Internet is also a maze of lead generation vendor sites designed to capture you and your information and turn it over to people who are paying to be introduced to you.

Some will take you directly to the information you want, while others will take you places you weren't sure you wanted to go.

Search engines like Google have programs that search the web for relevant sites pertaining to a given topic, such as "Chicago homes for sale," and deliver the addresses back to Google. Google then runs the results through an algorithm to make sure the sites are relevant to Google's search parameters.

But Google doesn't deliver free information for nothing. Pay-per-click is a new tool advertisers use to assure that they will land at the top of the search, so you may not be getting results as relevant as you think.

There's nothing wrong with skewing results in favor of profits, but as a consumer, you should know that shopping for homes on the Internet is a far cry from letting your fingers do the walking in the Yellow Pages.

One way to tell that you are dealing with a lead generation company is that you are likely to be required to give personal information about yourself before you are given access to the data you want, although some individual agents require this as well in order to screen lookers from legitimate buyers. With an advertisement, such as the listing presentations on REALTOR.com or the NAR-sponsored video clips at *Realty Times*, you can simply click on the agent's e-mail info or call them on the phone for more information.

If you are looking for a technology-proficient agent, however, using searches could be an excellent way to get introduced to one. Online agents are more likely to know technologies that will allow free and easy communication as well as quick access to listings.

Where Can I See the Most Homes?

The most listings at any time are available from your agent online. These will be the most up-to-date listings with the correct asking price and terms from the sellers. Your agent may even know of homes that are about to come on the market. The advantage of looking at homes online with your agent is that she may have personal knowledge about certain homes because she's been inside, and been inside other comparable homes for sale. That's invaluable to understanding why one home is marketed at one price while a very similar home may be higher or lower. Sellers vary in their need or desire to sell, and that individuality is reflected in the price of the home and its condition.

You don't want to waste your time looking at homes that aren't appropriate for your needs and wants. Rely on your agent to show you homes online via his own site, or through e-mail alerts about true contenders.

When you shop online, remember that you are looking at advertisements. Real estate agents pay for online exposure just as they would for newspaper print ads, so you will find a wide variety in the quality, style, and presentation of listings to the public.

In addition to REALTOR.com, which promotes NAR member listings free of charge, there are other places where you can view homes:

- HomePages.com integrates detailed home listings, bird's-eye views of neighborhoods, and comprehensive community and local amenity information. Operated by HouseValues, it is a lifestyle and neighborhood-centric site that combines community demographics, crime statistics, school details, parks and recreation, and local amenities and services with searchable aerial imagery.

- Craigslist.org offers classified ads to agents and FSBO sellers. Unlike MLS organizations, Craigslist does not monitor the ads but relies on users to report infractions, so buyer beware.

- FSBO sites, such as forsalebyowner.com and owners.com, are growing in popularity, but their coverage is still spotty because they rely on individuals to post their own listings. Owners must be willing to go to the time, trouble, and expense of marketing a home online. Some don't have the skills or the patience to provide robust information about their homes, so there will be a wide variance in the quality of the listings.

- Foreclosure.com tracks more than 1.2 million foreclosure, preforeclosure, bankruptcy, FSBO, and tax lien listings, providing the largest and most accurate searchable database of foreclosed homes and investment property.

- Oodle (www.oodle.com) is a new search engine for local classified ads and purports to have one of the nation's largest indexes of home listings in the 102 markets it serves. Listings include local listings that have been submitted to the MLS, for-sale-by-owner, and foreclosure listings.

- Trulia (www.trulia.com) is also new on the scene, and advertises itself as a property search engine for real estate agents and consumers. According to the web site, the searches do not include for-sale-by-owner properties.

■ Some local REALTOR® association or MLS sites provide a special display of properties listed in the MLS on their own web sites to encourage consumers to contact an agent if they want more information.

When you view homes on the Internet, keep in mind that you may be introduced to types of homes, neighborhoods, and price ranges that you wouldn't shop in otherwise. This exposure can lead you to want homes that are out of your price range or are impractical in some other way, but it doesn't hurt to see what the next level home offers in the way of amenities. When you do shop in your price range, you'll have a better idea of what is and isn't a good buy.

The Internet can be a great place to get ideas about neighborhoods, homes, and features you might not have considered otherwise. Use it wisely to eliminate as well as add to your shopping cart. That way, when you get ready to view homes in person, you'll be more able to make an informed decision and a better offer.

New versus Existing Homes

There are two major types of homes sold in the United States: new and existing. New homes are those offered for sale directly by builders, while existing homes (also known as resales) are homes that have had at least one owner. The National Association of

Home Builders (NAHB) tracks starts and completions of newly constructed homes, while the NATIONAL ASSOCIATION OF REALTORS® tracks the sales of existing homes.

Eighty-five percent of existing homes in the nation are sold through real estate professionals. While home buyers can purchase homes directly from builders, many choose to have an agent assist them in the process. About 13 percent of homes are sold by homeowners directly to buyers without the assistance of agent marketing. These are the FSBO properties.

Characteristics of new homes and existing homes vary somewhat due to the cultural, economic, and product advancements of the period the homes were built. In 1950, new homes serving the baby boom were built with about 1,000 square feet and offered two bedrooms and one bath. By 1975, a standard new home had about 1,535 square feet and cost $42,600. By 2005, both new and existing homes had skyrocketed to new records in both size and price. The NAHB predicts that by 2010, the typical new home will have 2,200 square feet and offer three or more bedrooms, two and a half baths, and a two-car or larger garage.

Clearly, houses are getting larger and consumers are getting more demanding about the features they want included. Consistently, new homes cost about 20 percent more than existing homes of comparable size and amenities. To approach the size, amenities, and fresh allure that new homes have, existing homes are often remodeled and updated, or they sell for considerably less unless some kind of demand such as location makes them sell at a premium. That is why, when price comparisons are made between new and existing homes, square footage is important but so is the cost of updates such as flooring, countertops, appliances, and interior design features.

Because of the natural growth of towns from their original business district—a downtown or square—older homes are typically closer in while newer homes are further out, not unlike rings of age on a tree. Older homes reflect the lifestyles of the times during which they were built, as you'll learn when you start looking at homes.

New Homes

According to the NAHB, new homes offer a number of advantages over existing homes.

More Amenities/Conveniences.   New homes feature newer and better materials, built-in appliances, high-speed data access, and better wiring than existing homes. The diminishing cost of some features such as whirlpool tubs in relationship to housing prices has allowed newer homes to include more amenities than many older homes.

Safety.   Occupants of new homes are almost six times less likely to die from fire than occupants of existing homes. Many new homes come equipped with hardwired smoke detectors on every level, complete with battery backup should the power go out. Fires are diminished due to the lack of need for space heaters and because of more efficient central heating systems and better insulation. Electrical power systems in new homes are properly sized for the heavier electrical demands of today's homes, and wiring systems are less likely to cause fires. Circuit breakers have replaced fuse boxes, which can be overloaded by using the wrong size fuse. Ground fault interrupters for bathrooms, kitchens, and outside receptacles reduce the chance of fire and electrocution. Today's glass in tub enclosures and patio doors in new homes must be tempered so that it will crumble if broken instead of shattering into large jagged pieces that can seriously injure people.

Health.   The building industry has responded to the health risks of certain products by building with products and systems that make new homes better for your health. Asbestos, which can increase the risk of respiratory disease, has been eliminated from shingles, pipe, cement board, roof tar, floor tiles, ceiling tiles, and insulation. Lead, a potential poison, is no longer used as an ingredient in paint or as solder for plumbing. Formaldehyde emissions from particle board and hardwood plywood have been greatly reduced in new homes. And urea-formaldehyde finishes on most kitchen cabinets are now baked or cured to minimize emissions. Builders are now installing systems to control radon gas, a known cancer-causing agent, where it is a problem. These systems usually include installation of gravel and polyethylene film beneath basement floors and concrete slabs, and provide for later installation of vent pipes and fans, if required. Older homes frequently have no gravel in which to collect the gas, no polyethylene film to retard movement of the gas through the slab, and no vent pipes. Mitigating radon from an existing home is generally far more expensive than building radon prevention techniques into a new home.

Energy Efficiency.   Because of better windows, more efficient heating and cooling equipment, better control of air infiltration, and greater use of insulation, new homes consume half as much energy as homes built prior to 1980. Homes built earlier tend to be drafty and less comfortable, and frost and condensation are more likely to appear on windows, drip down, and cause deterioration of wood trim and walls.

Lower Maintenance.   New homes can require less maintenance. New homes are available with siding, windows, and trim that seldom need painting. Wood decks are typically made of pressure-treated lumber resistant to rot and insects. Pressure-treated wood is also used where wood comes in contact with concrete.

In addition, you can customize a new home for some personal preferences and upgrade your selections for a more elegant finish before the home is built, which is less expensive than retrofitting an existing home because of tear-out costs.

Existing Homes

You'd get some argument against new homes being better from folks who love the charm and quality of materials that many existing homes offer. Existing homes are often beautiful, highly individual, and built of materials that would be prohibitive in cost today. In addition, they can occupy larger lots and better locations near central businesses and other attractions.

In an existing neighborhood, everything is already built. You can see what is around the corner, what services are nearby, and who your neighbors are. You can see what kind of growth is taking place, and you can review the comparables (similarly priced homes for sale in the same neighborhood), whereas comparables are more difficult to ascertain in new homes. You can see what kinds of updates are being done by other families to make the most of the space and what kinds of amenities they are adding.

There are several benefits to owning an existing home.

Hot Neighborhoods Net Full Recovery of Remodeling Costs.   If your neighborhood is being rediscovered by buyers, they may be more inclined to remodel an existing home if you can tell them that they may get 80 percent to more than 100 percent of their remodeling costs back. Improvements help the home, the neighborhood, and the community.

Negotiation.   Because of the low margins on new homes, there is very little opportunity for negotiation. The builder is more willing to market an unfinished home and sit on an unsold home to get the right price because he has more leverage. The average home owner may be in a must-sell position and may be more willing to deal on issues such as move-in dates or repairs, especially if the buyer insists on a repair allowance. That can provide needed cash to make repairs without your having to incur a home improvement loan right away.

Every Neighborhood Has Its Gems.   You can discover the adorable, cleverly updated, or beautifully maintained homes in just about any neighborhood. Drive around and look for the area amenities, such as community theaters with the visiting acting troupes, the dog park, the recreation center, and the little grocery that imports the best Australian wines and Greek olives.

Neighborhoods Are Made Good through the Commitment of Neighbors. As a buyer, you may be interested in making new friends and becoming part of something special. What better way to become part of the neighborhood than to join the local service league that adopts its schools and parks?

Ultimately, any buyer's decision will come down to what they want to spend on a home and improvements, access to work and services, and community amenities. There may be a lot to learn about a new neighborhood, where everything is shiny and still under development, but even so, an agent can be invaluable in helping you find out what is planned and how long community amenities will take to be completed.

Working with an agent can also be invaluable in an existing neighborhood, as many professionals make a point of farming certain areas so they know everything there is to know. They may have personal experience with many of the homes that have sold in the area, which can save you time and effort as you learn which areas are best for you and your family to explore.

Home Warranties

New homes will be under warranty by the builder for a given period, usually one or two years, but the warranty doesn't cover everything you may think it does. Because so many builders use subcontractors, they will refuse to cover work such as concrete for foundations and sidewalks. If a contractor puts too much water in the mix, you could have a brittle foundation. So be sure to ask what items are warrantied and which aren't. Separate warranties will be provided by appliance manufacturers. Reputable builders will make this aspect of home maintenance and management as painless as possible for home buyers by putting together resources that they can use, including a warranty department that handles claims.

For existing homes, there are home warranties that you can buy or that the seller can provide for you as an incentive that assists in the event that an appliance or system fails. Home warranties cover anything that is built into the house, from plumbing fixtures to cooktops. Moveable appliances such as refrigerators aren't covered unless you add them to your warranty under a separate rider.

The way warranties work is that when you experience a failure, such as the air-conditioning system failing to cool, you call the warranty company, and the warranty company calls the appropriate technician. In essence the warranty company serves as a referral system to deliver new business to participating plumbers, electricians, appliance repairmen, and so on. The technician calls you and sets up the repair appointment.

Warranties can be helpful, because when they are used, you only pay the deductible amount, but keep in mind that technicians are required to bring whatever they repair up to current code, which can require additional and substantial expense. Beware of technicians who pad your bill by selling you additional services that you may not need.

How Comprehensive Is Your Home Warranty?

Check your home warranty policy to see which of the following items are covered. Also check to see if the policy covers the full replacement cost of an item.

- Plumbing
- Electrical systems
- Water heater
- Furnace
- Heating ducts
- Water pump
- Dishwasher
- Stove/cooktop/ovens
- Microwave
- Refrigerator
- Washer/dryer
- Swimming pool (may be optional)

(Copyright 2006. Reprinted with permission from REALTOR® Magazine Online.)

Warranty companies are not designed to supply you with new appliances, air conditioners, or hot water heaters. Age, condition, and maintenance records are all crucial to any decision the warranty company makes about whether to pay for repairs. If the warranty company chooses to replace an appliance, it won't necessarily be the same maker or the same quality you had before.

Where warranties pay for themselves is in the replacement of components, which can fail on fairly new machines. For example, computer chips can fail but are easily replaced.

CHAPTER 6

Location, Location, Location

Finding the right home is only part of the home buying experience. As a homeowner, you'll be an active participant in your *neighborhood*. Depending on your life stage, you may be interested in schools and parks, local amenities, transportation, and other considerations that contribute to overall quality of life.

The most frequently cited reason for choosing the area for a home purchase in the *2005 NAR Profile of Home Buyers and Sellers* is "neighborhood quality." Among respondents' considerations was proximity of the neighborhood to their jobs, schools, friends, and family. Of less concern were the distances between their homes and public transportation, health facilities, airports, or entertainment venues, although those preferences changed with age, lifestyle, and personal interests.

Suburban or Urban?

Neighborhoods come with all kinds of characteristics. According to environmental psychologist and Design Institute of San Diego instructor David Kopec, Ph.D. (www.dakcalifornia.com), housing must "be able to meet people's physical and psychological needs, as well as provide them protection against weather and pollution." He suggests, "Housing preferences are driven by lifestyle factors such as family size, life stage, culture, and income."

The urban lifestyle is associated with city living, which is designed around the density of the population. Urban neighborhoods tend to be communities near central business districts in medium to large cities and feature more multifamily housing, including row houses, condominiums, and townhomes. Housing tends to be built upward (vertical) rather than horizontal, because of the high expense of buildable land.

Among the attractions to urban living are easy access to job centers and city amenities such as cultural centers, restaurants, and entertainment. Many communities have excellent public transportation to offset the higher costs of housing. Public parks and spaces become more important as residents sacrifice owning green spaces such as large yards and gardens in order to live closer to the inner city.

The downside of urban living is that density produces the side effects of noise, dirt, and crime, but many people thrive on the hustle, bustle, and excitement of city life.

Suburban neighborhoods are extensions of urban neighborhoods but offer more room for homes with less density. The suburban neighborhood revolves around schools, parks, and other amenities that support family life as something to be kept separate and apart from work. Depending on the strength of public transportation and roads, some bedroom communities can be fairly close to business districts while others require a lengthy commute by car or train. Bedroom communities, otherwise known as the suburbs, are designed to be retreats.

But only 39 percent of households have children under the age of 18, which means that the suburban experience might not be as fulfilling to many households, including young and older singles, empty nesters, and retirees.

With the rising costs of fuel, long commutes are expensive. Many home buyers are considering the inner city, or urban experience, where commute times to work are brief and they are within walking or public transportation distance to local clubs, restaurants, museums, and galleries. It's a "live and work" environment.

There is a definite trend back to the city, NAR found in its most recent survey of home buyers and sellers. The survey noted a trend toward home buyers overall moving to urban areas. In 2003, sales in urban areas made up 17 percent of the market. In

2004, this number dipped slightly to 16 percent, but was back to 17 percent in 2005.

What these numbers show is that home buyers are looking to satisfy immediate housing needs, and they aren't necessarily looking at the home that they buy today as the home they will have tomorrow.

According to Kopec, the ideal location of one's home "will probably switch over time between urban and suburban environments, or suburban and rural environments."

"'Location, location, location,' depends greatly upon the person," says Dr. Kopec. "Because preferred locations depend greatly upon the services and opportunities available at that given point in one's life, location preferences often change with our growth and development. Perhaps the best guide for selecting the best location is understanding that most humans like to be around others who are like-minded in some way: children seeking playmates, academics seeking stimulation, yuppies seeking jobs, or simply people needing people with similar life experiences."

Finding the Right Neighborhood for You

You may be familiar enough with your area that you have in mind an ideal place to live. Perhaps you have friends or family there. Or you may be enticed by new homes and schools being developed in faraway suburbs. Maybe you're an urban pioneer and relish the thought of transforming blighted neighborhoods into walking communities with lofts, brownstones, dog parks, and coffee houses. It all depends on what you value.

As mentioned earlier, most home buyers view neighborhood quality as the most important factor. Other factors influencing their choices were:

- Proximity to jobs/school
- Proximity to friends/family
- School district
- Shopping
- Parks/recreation
- Planned community
- Entertainment venues
- Public transportation
- Proximity to airport
- Health facilities

Whatever your reasons for choosing a neighborhood and home type, there are some great ways to learn what's available so you can narrow your selection.

Over 90 percent of home buyers used an agent while searching for their home, but most home buyers also utilize a number of other resources, including the Internet, to find a home. Because of the robust, interactive nature of the Internet, many home buyers engage their agents to help them find a home and use the Internet to select homes to visit in person, or they use the Internet to eliminate unsuitable homes.

Learning about Neighborhoods Online

If you want to find out some information on your own, there are many ways to learn more about neighborhoods online. Thanks to Internet technologies, you can peruse neighborhoods almost as easily as homes online.

Almost all web sites such as REALTOR.com that have listings to view also have links to neighborhood information, often including satellite photos. Using zip codes, many online sites have state-of-the-art satellite technology combined with detailed information about homes, neighborhoods, and nearby conveniences and services. This helps buyers and sellers to use their computers to do detailed research about houses and neighborhoods before ever actually setting foot in a for-sale home. You can get an aerial map of the entire zip code, with an overview of the homes for sale and where they are, as well as neighborhood parks and other amenities. Another resource, overlooked by many consumers, is city or municipal web sites and local agent web sites, which may highlight neighborhoods that would not be known to buyers otherwise.

The biggest problem that neighborhoods face is that many are only known colloquially, which is one reason why so many online searches for neighborhoods and homes use zip codes. But zip codes don't tell the whole story. A zip code may be large enough to include one school you want for your children and another one you don't want. You need to know *which* home is in *which* school district. That's where your agent is invaluable in saving you time, because he will show you only the homes that are within your neighborhood parameters as well as your price range.

Another way you can find out about neighborhoods is to visit *Realty Times'* Market Conditions Reports® on REALTOR.com. Key in the name of the city you're interested in and a list of participating agent-reporters will pop up, each with their own perspectives of what's happening in local markets. The advantage to searching on Market Conditions Reports is that the agents list their neighborhoods by name as well as by zip code. Look for other areas listed by the agents and click on them to find out market conditions for those communities. Be sure to e-mail them and ask questions, if you don't already have an agent. Find out what they know about local communities, the best schools, and more.

Shopping for Neighborhoods in Person

The neighborhood you choose can have a big impact on your lifestyle—safety, available amenities, and convenience all play their part. And there is no better way to learn about a neighborhood than by visiting it.

Tips for Finding
the Perfect Neighborhood

- *Make a list of the activities—movies, health club, church—you engage in regularly and stores you visit frequently.* See how far you would have to travel from each neighborhood you're considering to engage in your most common activities.

- *Check out the school district.* The Department of Education in your town can probably provide information on test scores, class size, percentage of students who attend college, and special enrichment programs. If you have school-age children, also consider paying a visit to schools in the neighborhoods you're considering. Even if you don't have children, a house in a good school district will be easier to sell in the future.

- *Find out if the neighborhood is safe.* Ask the police department for neighborhood crime statistics. Consider not only the number of crimes but also the type—burglaries, armed robberies—and the trend of increasing or decreasing crime. Also, is crime centered in only one part of the neighborhood, such as near a retail area?

- *Determine if the neighborhood is economically stable.* Check with your local city economic development office to see if income and property values in the neighborhood are stable or rising. What is the percentage of homes to apartments? Apartments don't necessarily diminish value, but they do mean a more transient population. Do you see vacant businesses or homes that have been for sale for months?

(Continued)

Tips for Finding
the Perfect Neighborhood *(Continued)*

- *See if you'll make money.* Ask a local REALTOR® or call the local REALTOR® association to get information about price appreciation trends in the neighborhood. Although past performance is no guarantee of future results, this information may give you a sense of how good an investment your home will be. A REALTOR® or the government planning agency also may be able to tell you about planned developments or other changes in the neighborhood—like a new school or highway—that might affect value.

- *See for yourself.* Once you've narrowed your focus to two or three neighborhoods, go there and walk around. Are homes tidy and well maintained? Are streets quiet? Pick a warm day if you can and chat with people working or playing outside. Are they friendly? Are there children to play with your family?

(Copyright 2006. Reprinted with permission by REALTOR® Magazine Online.)

Here are some additional tips to get a feel for what it would be like living among your new neighbors:

- Talk to the neighbors of homes you visit. Ask them what they like about the area and what they would like to see changed. Ask them about the best schools, restaurants, parks, and so on.

- Drive around the neighborhood at different times of the day and night, particularly at peak traffic times, and try out the neighbors' suggestions for places to eat, shop, and play. Were they right?

- Drive to and from your work to the neighborhoods you like best. Which commutes take the longest? Can you live with more time on the road?

- Look at how neighbors maintain their homes, and you'll find a good indicator of the homeowners' attitudes.

- Examine your own attitudes. Are you willing to maintain your new home to the standards your neighbors have set for mowing, shoveling snow, and the like? If not, you might be in for some friction.

- Have in mind at least three things you must have in your neighborhood and three things that you do not want, and see how the neighborhood matches up.

Finding the Right Schools

Keep in mind that real estate professionals may be prohibited from offering you certain information that could be construed as steering you to or away from a particular neighborhood. Providing information or opinions on the quality of schools is one of those topics. However, your agent can direct you to places where you can peruse school district information and make comparisons yourself.

One way to find out is by looking at homes on REALTOR.com and scrolling down to the additional information, which will include the elementary, middle, and high schools in the home's district.

You can also compare schools online by using a search engine such as Google (www.google.com). Fill in your city name and "schools." (For example, enter "Phoenix schools.") This should take you to the local school district, where you can look up the statistics of the schools you've been introduced to. You can also contact the schools directly for more information. Your state will most likely have a web site dedicated to school districts as well.

View your top school choices and get a feel for the teaching culture and administration and how students and parents fit in. Find out the school's state test scores and rankings online, or visit the principal and staff in person. You may find you adjust or specifically target your housing choices based on this research.

Homefair.com, an online relocation guide and resource center, is full of information including salary calculators, apartments for rent, retirement choices, weather, and a myriad of other data you'd like to know about your new city or neighborhood. The reports on local schools and child care centers are free, as well as the city reports, which offer side-by-side comparisons of two cities' cost of living, climate, demographics, and other vital information from a database that is kept current with quarterly updates, says the site.

Fair Housing Laws

The sale and rental of housing is a state-regulated process, but assuring equal housing opportunity in transactions is overseen by the U.S. Department of Housing and Urban Development (www.hud.gov).

Fair housing and equal opportunity (FHEO) is a right you have that is protected by the government. You have the right to expect that housing will be available to you without discrimination or other limitations based on race, color, religion, sex, handicap, familial status, or national origin. This includes the right to expect:

- Housing in your price range made available to you without discrimination.

- Equal professional service.

- The opportunity to consider a broad range of housing choices.

- No discriminatory limitations on communities or locations of housing.

- No discrimination in the financing, appraising, or insuring of housing.

- Reasonable accommodations in rules, practices, and procedures for persons with disabilities.

- Nondiscriminatory terms and conditions for the sale, rental, financing, or insuring of a dwelling.

- To be free from harassment or intimidation for exercising your fair housing rights.

Safety

Most everyone has a different opinion of what constitutes a safe neighborhood. If you're concerned whether a neighborhood is safe or not, visit the local police station and ask to meet with the officers in charge of patrols. It won't hurt to get on a first-name basis with the men and women who protect your neighborhood, and the patrol officers can also give you some perspective.

To find some interesting statistics on cities, including crime statistics, take a look at Homefair, at www.homefair.com. You can also get crime indexes for thousands of U.S. cities and Canada.

While you can get an overview online, nothing takes the place of walking through the neighborhood you're interested in, and meeting and talking with the individuals who serve your neighbors.

Commutes

The bigger your family, the more you have to consider your schedule as well as their activities. Can you reasonably get home from work in time to get your child to baseball practice? Dance lessons? Tutoring? These days, many adults and children are overscheduled, and the longer you are commuting, the more frustrating your life may seem.

That's another consideration when choosing a neighborhood. How close are you to all the places you need to be—work, friends, family, activities, parks, shopping, services, health care, and entertainment? Think about whether moving further away from work is worth it if you have to also give up your favorite dry cleaners, exercise studio, or grocery store.

One idea is to schedule an experimental week in your day planner, crammed with your typical appointments, including haircuts, doctor visits, and Little League. Test-drive these locations from your intended neighborhood at the time of day you would actually perform these errands during your work week.

Only you and your family can make the decision whether closer in or further out is the right direction to go.

Compromise on Size or Price

The choice of neighborhood is so important that most home buyers are least likely to compromise on neighborhood quality. One-third of home buyers find the home they wanted in the price range they want to pay, according to NAR, but the vast majority of home buyers compromise on something—the size of the home they purchase, buying a home a greater distance from work/school, the condition of the home, lot size, and planned expenditures such as furnishings, remodeling, and appliances.

Be prepared, when you start looking at neighborhoods and homes, to make some compromise because no home—not even a brand-new luxury home—will exactly match your criteria. There will always be some feature you need or want that a single residence simply can't supply.

The best way to shop for a home is to think about the majority of features you would like a neighborhood and home to have, and start there. Be willing to compromise on items you know you can live with or without. Choose the surroundings first, and the right home will appear.

CHAPTER 7

Buying a Newly Constructed Home

The thrill of buying a brand-new home that no one has ever lived in before is that, in many cases, it can be built the way you want it, according to your means and the builder's ability. There's also something exciting about going to a brand-new neighborhood or subdivision and being part of the future of the new area.

It's tempting to jump in the car and tour new neighborhoods that are being created by developers and builders. New communities and homes can offer the latest in lifestyle concepts. Where else would you see grand condominium hotels or senior retirement communities complete with golf courses, swimming pools, and dance floors? If you want to see a number of homes that might specifically meet your needs, such as garden homes (limited yard sizes) or luxury homes, a new home community can give you a lot of information. They are also fun to tour for the latest in interior design and decorating ideas, not to mention the latest in technologies and appliances.

Builders Are Businesspeople

One reason why home buyers enjoy cruising new homes is that they can do so somewhat anonymously, without worrying about disturbing a homeowner. Builders make home buyers feel welcome with open models that are decorated with the latest ideas, fixtures, and appliances, so buyers get the double benefit of seeing how current their new home can really look.

But you're not as anonymous as you think. Builders or their representatives will ask you for your name and address, so they can follow up with you. Getting visitor information is also part of security procedures.

Sometimes home buyers think that if they find the home they want, they can ask the builder to reduce the price of the home by the amount of the commission that would have been paid to their real estate agent. That strategy rarely works.

If you have an agent but tour an open house or model home without her, or without presenting her card to the builder or builder's salesperson, you might miss the opportunity to have your agent represent you should you want to purchase one of the homes you see. Many builders will refuse to pay an agent who comes back after the fact and demands a commission. The builder can rightfully ask, why weren't you with your client? However, many builders are happy to pay your agent a commission because it may bring them more business in the future. But beware that you may inadvertently cut your agent out of the negotiations by speaking to the builder on your own.

One of the biggest fallacies of new home buying is that you'll save money if you negotiate on your own. Nothing could be further from the truth. Your agent can actually save you money and trouble down the road by advising you of many items you need to know, from negotiating upgrades with the builder to move-in day.

Many agents specialize in new home construction sales and know the ins and outs of buying a new home. Many builders have sale agreement forms drawn up by their own attorneys for use on their new home products. These forms may not have consumer language in them concerning things that a buyer might assume are covered, such as inspection clauses and warranty information. That's reason enough to have your agent with you!

You also want to know if some builders are offering incentives or why they aren't. Your agent can explain the market conditions. She can also help you avoid overbuying or underbuying in a given community. For example, you may be tempted to buy a modest home and add on too many upgrades, which may make your home more difficult to resell. You may be better off buying a more expensive home in another community because the other comparable homes will help keep the value of your home higher. Remember, although builders make money on upgrades, you may not. Not all upgrades pay for themselves.

Let your agent call builders in advance and introduce you as her client. That way, when you go and sign the guestbook or present your agent's card, the builder and builder's representative will know that you have representation and be better prepared to serve you.

Choosing a Builder

It's important to you to work with a builder who has a fine reputation for customer service as well as the quality product he builds.

The National Association of Home Builders (NAHB), like NAR, is an organization that holds its members to a high standard of performance and ethics. It provides educational opportunities and certifications to assure that its members meet the highest quality standards in home building. It takes a dedicated professional to keep up with the latest advancements in construction techniques, codes, and standards—structural design, materials, energy conservation, fire safety, electrical, plumbing, heat and air code updates, indoor air quality and ventilation, acoustics, environmental features, consumer preferences, and so much more.

In addition, you want to make sure that your builder is expert in the type of home you want to build, so that they have the resources and experience to deliver the best product possible for the money.

Types of Builders

According to the NAHB there are two basic types of builders—custom and production.

Custom home builders generally:

- Build on land you own. Some custom builders also build on land they own.
- Build one-of-a-kind houses. A custom home is a site-specific home built from a unique set of plans for a specific client. Some custom builders may offer design/build services.
- Build single-family homes.
- Are small-volume builders (25 or fewer homes a year).
- Tend to build high-end homes.

Production home builders generally:

- Build on land they own.
- Tend to use stock plans, but usually offer a variety of plan choices and options.
- Build all types of housing—single-family, condos, town houses, and rental properties.
- Are large-volume builders (more than 25 homes a year).
- Build for all price points—entry level, move-up, luxury, and so on.

Five Factors to Consider in Choosing a Home Builder

To choose a builder, consider the following suggestions from the NAHB.

1. *Reputation.* As you did when you chose your agent, ask any friends and family who have built a new home if they are happy with their builder. If your agent isn't familiar with the builder, you can ask the builder for references or check out his references online.

2. *Area.* You want to make sure your builder is familiar with local building laws so that you aren't hit with impact fees or other fees you weren't expecting. It may come as a shock to find out that in addition to your new home, you may also have to fund streetlights, street paving, or other expenses. If your state requires home builders to be licensed, you will want to check the license status of your builder and inquire as to filed complaints or other problems with the licensing entity or contractor's board.

3. *Type of home.* Does the builder specialize in the kind of home you want? Can you see other examples of the style and design you want in other communities? Does the builder have a spec home or model home for you to view?

4. *Warranties.* One advantage to buying new is having warranties on certain construction and appliances. Does your builder guarantee beyond standard warranties? Most problems should show up within the first year.

5. *Financial strength.* You want a builder who can weather unforeseen conditions such as rain delays, construction cost increases, and far-in-the-future completions and who will be around for the long haul.

Production builders will tend to concentrate in metropolitan areas, where there will be huge differences in the types of homes offered as well as the quality of construction and price points.

In some cases, you might find the distinction between custom and production builders confusing as the latter have created divisions where they do some customization of their products. These builders might be called semi-custom builders. For example, a production builder may offer a floor plan at a certain price in a community, but if you want to modify the plan (move or add walls, baths, fireplaces, or other features) then you are customizing the plan.

What will make a difference to your interaction with the builder is whether you own your own property. A custom builder may have in-house plans that he can build on your property and/or may customize existing plans for your site features.

Searching for a Builder Online

The NAHB web site (NAHB.org) provides tutorials on how to get a home built, but you can also find members in your area to interview by going to www.NAHB.org, clicking on "Find Your Local Builders' Association" (under "Resources"), and entering the state or zip code for the area you're interested in.

Another web site, www.Move.com, is an advertising site where builders can show their communities, model homes, floor plans, site plans, and brand identity to consumers. The site has a number of ways to search for homes, including:

- Single family: stand-alone dwellings with land included.
- Condo/townhomes: attached housing with two or more units; community amenities; low maintenance; HOA fees are usual.
- Active adult community: age-restricted housing, generally geared for 55 years of age or older with community rules that maintain the development as age-requirement oriented.
- Build on your lot: You own the lot or are willing to buy a lot, or buy a lot from the builder for a custom or production home.

You can also search by zip code, city and state, and price range. To help you with your selection, Move.com has segmented large metropolitan areas into adjoining suburbs and towns, so searches are much easier, especially if you don't happen to know the zip code of the area you want to go. You can check the boxes of the municipalities you're interested in to save time. Many homes have virtual tours, floor plans, and community information.

You can search for homes at www.Newhomesource.com, a web site produced by a consortium of top builders including nationally known builders such as Pulte, Centex, Lennar, Beazer, David Weekley Homes, and more. Home searches are easy: Just key in the city, state, and price range, and a world of homes will pop up, including homes already built and planned homes. The site also lists which builders participate in the area, so if you are moving from another city and want to see if your favorite builder is working in your new town, you can find out in which communities and at what price ranges they're building.

Newspapers

You can also look in the homes section of the newspaper for the latest projects and homes for sale. Be sure to make a list of builders who build the type of home you want in the price range you're looking for, and show the list to your agent. Compare the list with builders and homes your agent recommends, and you might find some projects and builders in common to visit.

What Kinds of New Homes Are Available?

Production builders as well as many custom builders produce several types of inventory for buyers to see.

Spec homes are homes that are built for sale on the speculation that a buyer will purchase the home and move right in. Often, spec homes are offered through an association with a local agent, so even though no one has lived in the home, the builder can take advantage of the agent's marketing. If the builder markets the home, the property will not be featured in the local MLS, and in many newspapers it will only be advertised in the "new homes" section of the paper.

Model homes are typical of homes in the builder's community. They are also built on spec, but the difference is that the builder, builder representative, or other sales team members may use the home during daylight hours as an office and sales center in order to sell other homes in the community built by the builder. Many embellish the model with custom features such as upgrades in appliances, paints, or materials, so when you view a model home be sure to compare the upgrades with the home you are interested in building or buying. Other builders do the opposite and build the model as it would appear with no upgrades, reserving upgrades for add-ons.

Model homes are typically not sold to the public until the builder is ready to move out of the community. In some cases, the model home might be sold to a buyer through a rent-back agreement where the builder continues to occupy the home for a period of time. If you are interested in buying a model home, make sure that other homeowners in the community have also purchased upgrades, or you may find yourself slightly over-improved for the market.

Some builders purchase lots or homes that they tear down in order to *build to suit* a home for the buyer. This strategy is only successful in rapidly appreciating markets or markets with many homes that are in desirable locations, but functionally obsolete. In this case, the builder buys for *lot value*, which means that the land is valuable but the structure or home is so outdated, troubled, or obsolete that it has no more value to the marketplace. This, of course, is a matter of opinion, as many homes may be torn down that still have useful lives but simply do not appeal to the new buyer. The builder may have plans to show the buyer, which can be modified for the buyer's preferences, or the buyer may have plans of their own.

Working with Builder Representatives

When you enter a model home or a building site's portable office, you will most likely be greeted by a builder's representative or salesperson. You need to remember that the salesperson represents the builder, not you. You are a customer, and the salesperson will do her best to serve you, but her job is to sell you a home.

This is the point where your agent will step back and let the salesperson take over, and this is as it should be. Your agent will listen, learn, and help you compare benefits, costs, and other considerations when you are ready to decide on a home. Your agent will also look out for your interests when it comes to reviewing the builder's contract. Some points will be negotiable, and your agent will help you decide what is in your best interest.

The builder's representative shows you the features of available homes in either standing inventory or homes to be built, and helps the buyer in the selection of the home's appointments. Typically, on-site representatives are not licensed real estate agents and may not be members of the local MLS.

Some builders also have greeters who register visitors such as walk-in buyers or buyers accompanied by agents. Greeters perform other tasks and functions that do not involve quoting prices, loan rates, or other discussions that may affect a forthcoming contract for purchase.

Some builders have in-house lending through which they will offer special discounts and rebates on your purchase, such as paying for the title policy or giving you cash back at closing if you use their lender. As with any loan, make sure to review the contract carefully to ensure that you are getting the best deal for your budget. The in-house lenders may simply raise the interest rate slightly in order to cover your so-called free title policy or other gift.

You may grow confused as you begin to wonder which person is working in your best interest. What you should expect is for your agent to be expert in new communities, builders and their reputations, new home contracts, basic construction terms and techniques, comparables and general pricing (e.g., what should an upgrade for hardwood floors or granite counters cost?), and keeping you from getting into a situation that can do you financial harm.

It is the builder's representative's job to sell you on the home and the community, and to be familiar with the infrastructure, roads, easements, and building restrictions. As a salesperson, the representative should be the ultimate authority on the builder's products, but she should also do an excellent job in counseling you, facilitating your transaction, and making you feel valued as a customer.

In order to assist you, the builder's representative has to find out your needs and preferences. Be prepared for questions like how did you hear about us? Are we in your price range? Have you looked at other communities? How soon do you plan to move? Do you have any special needs?

Being prepared for these questions is one thing, but be cautious about revealing too much information about yourself. Keep the conversation squarely on the builder's property, its features, and their guarantees. The reason? So you don't inadvertently reveal something about yourself that could damage your offer to buy. It is your agent's role to sell the builder on why your offer should be accepted. In return, the representative should be able to tell you about the builder, the homes, what construction methods are used, and unique features.

Dena Mentis, a builder/developer, consultant, and author (www.newhomesmedia.com), says, "If you have questions about the 'lay of the land,' the sales consultant should be able to answer questions about soils, grading, home placement, home site sizes, neighborhood rules and limitations set forth by the city, special taxes, new home warranty parameters, and be the quintessential expert on where all the services and retail/commercial centers are in the area. Schools are an important subject; names and numbers of principals and district offices should be available to you."

The builder representative should also be familiar with any incentives the builder is offering, even if that is related to financing. "She should be able to sit down and discuss a general and updated accounting of various loan programs, interest rates, down payment requirements, and qualifying ratios before handing you off," suggests Mentis.

You may also be shown the terms of the purchase agreement, which should be explained to you in clear terms. "Your rights and well as the builder's are an important factor in a new home purchase," says Mentis. "Other facts and disclosures about the homes, area, taxes, and fees will be revealed at this time if they have not already surfaced." If you wish to, you can consult a real estate attorney before signing.

Once you have signed on the dotted line, the builder's sales consultant job is not over. "The process of having your home built to your agreed-upon specifications should be as hassle-free as possible," says Mentis. "The builder rep interfaces with the building superintendent, the design center manager, the lender's agent, the escrow company, and a host of others who work behind the scenes to complete your home."

Between the builder representative and your agent, you should be shielded from any unpleasant surprises.

Your Delivery Date

Because there are so many variables in building—supplies, weather, labor shortages, and other potential problems—your builder may not be able to deliver your home exactly on the appointed date. You may inadvertently cause delays by asking the builder to perform tasks that aren't in the original agreement, such as switching flooring or other materials.

To keep abreast of your home's progress, you should have meetings scheduled with the builder's representative and perhaps other staff such as project managers. The builder should outline clear dates by which you can expect the builder to perform certain functions, as well as dates for you to perform such things as finalizing selections, paying for upgrades, and walk-through inspections for pre-drywall, pre-settlement, and day-of-settlement inspections.

These are occasions when your agent should accompany you to represent your interests should anything be wrong or delayed. Many items should be required to be corrected in time for closing; if not, they should be covered under the warranty period that the builder guarantees.

Costs

Be prepared to pay more for new homes than ever before. An unprecedented set of circumstances have converged to make new home construction much more expensive—rising demand for new construction, rising fuel costs, and limited availability of materials if any natural disasters strike.

- Land is more expensive. Many growing communities have caught on to the fact that they can make their new neighbors pay for expansion costs with impact fees. Costs for new roads, sewers, and other services that may be used by the whole community are directly assessed to new homes, causing builders to pass along the fees to their customers. With property values increasing, property taxes are also increasing.

- The costs of home building materials have risen due to shortages in supplies, production disruptions due to natural disasters, and increased demands due to the hot real estate market.

- For years, builders have complained about the availability of skilled labor, causing many to pay trusted supervisors and leading craftsmen premium salaries to keep them on staff.

- Consumers are demanding more amenities, including more square footage to accommodate home offices, flex rooms, and more bedrooms; higher-end appliances and finishes; and wiring for electronics and high-speed Internet access, security systems, and more.

- In order to find buildable lots and to keep homes attractively affordable for first-time home buyers and others, most builders turn to the suburbs of major cities, where city planners work with them to develop new neighborhoods. While you may pay less for a brand new home, you may find that transportation costs are much higher.

Controlling Costs

If you're buying a model home, the builder will outline the upgrades that were done for the home, which may include items that aren't part of the base price of other homes for sale, such as backyard landscaping, extra lighting, more expensive appointments, and so on.

If you aren't buying the model but are purchasing a similar home, don't expect prices to be the same. You may want every upgrade you saw in the model, but your lot may cost more. Building materials may also cost more. Remember that the builder is able to buy in bulk, so an upgraded countertop might cost you less if you let the builder do it than it would if you installed it on your own. Plus you have the added benefit of having the work already done.

In a model home, the builder may include items that aren't in his normal inventory, such as window coverings. Again, you can price the item with another vendor or simply take it "as is." When you do take possession, the builder should ensure that the home is delivered in move-in condition by doing repairs and touch-ups due to wear from using the home as a sales office.

Keep notes of all the upgrades you would like to have, and compare homes that already include such amenities in the base price. You might find you end up paying less for a home in a more expensive community if you buy the base model, than if you buy a home in a less expensive community and add upgrade after upgrade.

Decide what is a must-have and what you can live without. Talk to your agent about which features and amenities will help you later when it comes time to sell your new home, as this could go a long way in helping you decide what to put in. Negotiating upgrades in your initial sales contract will save you extra change-order costs that builders use when items are changed after contract.

Deposits and Draws

You will typically be required to make a deposit when you sign your purchase agreement, and to fund upgrades before closing. Most builders will require you to pay for upgrades in advance of closing so that should you default for some reason, they will already have been paid and can negotiate with the next buyer. You won't get your money back. If you follow through to closing, your deposits and upgrades can be credited as down payment monies.

If you are building a custom home, your lender will provide the builder with a schedule of draws, money he can use to pay for materials and workers.

Negotiations

Your ability to negotiate price, amenities, and other factors will depend on the kind of market you're in. Like other sellers, builders are subject to market conditions. When conditions favor the seller with lots of available buyers and escalating prices, the builder will be less likely to negotiate or provide incentives. When the builder has sitting inventory, he might be more willing to negotiate because carrying costs add up. Even so, the builder might not take much off the asking price, but he might be more willing to throw a few incentives in such as free upgrades.

With a custom home, you've already agreed to the price because the home is being built for you, so there is much less negotiating room. However, your builder might be willing to put in an extra shelf here and there for you.

But a new home that hasn't sold costs the builder money every day it sits. If there is anything about the home that is less desirable than others, such as lot size or square footage, then the builder has some horse-trading to do. Keep an eye out for "builder close-outs." That's when the builder is getting ready to exit the community and still has some standing inventory or homes under completion that haven't sold.

This is an area where your agent can be helpful. Tell the agent what homes interest you, and let her do your negotiating. Sometimes it pays to move quickly, such as securing the best lot or the end unit, but if those opportunities are already gone, then you can turn the remaining inventory into a negotiating advantage.

Just be sure you're ready to act quickly should the builder say yes! Have your financing secured and your down payment money ready.

New Construction Home Buying Tips

- Visit homes in several different communities with your agent.

- Research builders online.

- Compare prices, construction quality, drive-up appeal, location, and amenities.

- Try to meet the builder or the supervisor who will oversee the construction of your home. Ask about experience.

- Ask for as much material as you can so you can familiarize yourself with the builder's policies, warranties, homeowner's manual, and other information.

- Be careful visiting your home while it's under construction. The property doesn't officially belong to you yet, so you might be considered a trespasser. Find out about your visitation rights and be careful. Construction sites can be dangerous whether workers are present or not.

Special Section: Manufactured Homes

According to the April 2005 National Modular Housing Council report, factory-built homes are more popular than ever, and will continue to be if the industry can continue to overcome outdated notions by home buyers, builders, and real estate agents as to their benefits.

Manufactured housing is built in a factory and transported in modules to the building site, while so-called "stick-built" homes are built by builders on the site from the foundation up.

Today, manufactured houses come in a wide range of modular plans and materials, and are used to make complete homes on residential building sites, or are sold in modular parts to speed stick-built housing along. Manufactured homes can cost less than half of what site-built homes with similar features cost.

Not only are builders increasingly using modular parts like trusses and walls in on-site building, but they are finding that building with manufactured parts can save on weather-related delays, theft of materials, labor problems, quality control, and other concerns. In addition, new innovations in technologies and delivery systems mean that manufactured and modular homes can be aesthetically competitive with site-built homes, including such features as nine-foot ceilings and roof pitches similar to site-built homes. With the addition of foundations, garages, porches, and decks, manufactured homes can blend seamlessly into existing neighborhoods of site-built homes.

"Today's factory-built homes are often hard to distinguish from site-built homes because they are constructed with the same materials and features such as bay windows and permanent foundations with garages and porches," says Mark Brunner, spokesperson for the Minnesota Manufactured Housing Association (MMHA). "Like site builders, factory builders offer hundreds of floor plans to customize with options like fireplaces, whirlpool tubs, walk-in closets, and tray ceilings."

The difference between *manufactured* homes and *modular* homes is a matter of codes. Manufactured homes meet federal codes, and modular homes meet state codes, but they are both factory-built. Every factory-built home must pass a rigorous inspection, says the MMHA, and meet the state and federal standards before it leaves the factory. The federal building code, often referred to as the "HUD Code," is a performance-based building code that regulates the construction of manufactured homes. Modular homes are built to state codes, or the International Residential Code (IRC).

The advantage for home buyers is that the product has to pass federal code and is labeled as such. Generally, the federal code is more flexible and allows more innovation than state codes, but both are strict about such items as ventilation, flame spread, structural loads, window construction, vapor retarders, and service wiring.

One of the most important hurdles to wider acceptance of manufactured housing is financing. Manufactured homes, like log homes and other specialty home building products, are not conventional, and lenders use conventional guidelines to approve loans. But more and more lenders are offering loans to allow manufactured homes to be built as single-family owned parcels.

Modular home production has increased nationally as well, with 42,700 homes built in 2004, up 13 percent from 37,800 in 2003, and more sales expected in 2005 and 2006 as building prices escalate. Fueling this growth is a combination of low interest rates, a push from the federal and local governments for more affordable housing, and a growing consumer awareness that the quality of factory construction offers many advantages over site-built homes.

However, manufactured homes are not accepted everywhere. Make sure the community you are building in has no restrictions on using modular housing. Check with municipal officials to see if the lot location allows modular homes.

CHAPTER 8

Buying an Existing Home

Like the age rings of a tree, neighborhoods can tell you a lot about past American culture. For discussion's sake, we'll assume that most cities grew the fastest after the immigration age of the late nineteenth century.

Close to downtown, where homeowners could hop the trolley to get to work, you may find your historical tour begins with Victorian gingerbread homes or plain-Jane rooming houses. Next you see the homes of the early twentieth century—the arts and crafts homes on large boulevards, the prairie homes, and the art deco–inspired beaux arts homes. Later, in the 1930s and 1940s, you might see street after street of charming Tudor-style homes with original stained glass still in place. Then came the postwar ranch-style homes where housing was long and sleek, and yards were big for baby boom children to play in.

Later new neighborhoods reflected the diversity of the times, with zero-lot-line homes for commuters, condos for singles, and so on. By the 1990s, there were all kinds of homes in all kinds of eclectic styles available to home buyers.

The point is that each of these housing style eras represents the culture, economy, and home buying preferences of the times, and the neighborhoods continue to be appreciated by home buyers today.

Your Investment in an Existing Home

By understanding the age of the homes you are looking at, you can appreciate what was going on at the time in the nation's culture. It's interesting to see how homes have changed to suit the times.

But you're living today—how can you shop for an existing home and make it work for you now?

Existing homes can be less expensive than newly constructed homes, as you may find by comparing new homes to existing homes of similar sizes and amenities. New homes usually cost more than similar existing homes by about 20 percent.

But this isn't always true. Existing homes can be more expensive than new homes because of period moldings, millwork, and other architectural details. If they are close to downtown areas with urban growth boundaries, they can be highly desirable. Existing homes are significantly cheaper than new homes if they are run-down and in need of expensive rehabilitation, but these are hard to find in good areas.

Let's explore further advantages of existing homes:

- *Existing* doesn't mean *old*. An existing home can be one year old or less. It just means it's been lived in by a homeowner.

- Existing homes generally have easy proximity to jobs, shopping, and services.

- Most existing homes are in established neighborhoods—what you see is what you get.

- It is easy to find comparables on existing homes, which carry better histories of home sales so you can know what the fair market value is.

- Sellers of existing homes may be more open to negotiation. Builders pay the most recent prices for lots and materials; homeowners who have occupied their home for years may have more room to negotiate price and terms.

- There is a greater probability of revitalization in existing neighborhood areas. Sooner or later land values will prove irresistible to developers; the remodeling of a nearby shopping center can boost nearby home prices, while new neighborhoods are always competing with even newer neighborhoods.

- Existing homes can be charming. Some materials such as vintage stained glass or all-wood stairs can't be duplicated today without tremendous costs.

■ An existing home that needs work can be a bargain, especially if you put in sweat equity; you can create what you want.

In other words, you may get into a neighborhood when prices are lazy, and suddenly your house is hot! That can only happen in existing neighborhoods with older homes. In new communities, whenever you buy new you are paying the latest price, and equity is more likely to build over time, because buyers can always buy brand-new next door or down the street. It will take time for the neighborhood to be built out before resales can make money.

It's competition from new homes that sellers of existing homes have to worry about. They're competing with updated floor plans, new appliances, and luxury finishes that weren't available to previous generations of homes.

You have a lot of choice with existing homes—there's more inventory, and you can either buy one already remodeled or do the updates yourself. You can have your cake and granite countertops, too.

Shopping for an Existing Home

When you shop for a home in an established neighborhood, look at the home closely, but be open to the possibilities for improvement. Imagine your furniture sprucing up the interior—doesn't it look better already? With the same eye toward change, think of the homes you are viewing with a fresh coat of paint or updated countertops.

That's asking a lot, but that is what it might take for you to see the room for improvement that can bring you a higher price when it comes time for resale. The better a home is updated, the better the resale possibilities.

If you are interested in a certain vintage, like 1930s Tudor cottages, ask your agent where the best selection of such homes is available and consider the neighborhood. Is it close to work centers, hospitals, shopping centers? City infrastructure will help the home retain its value.

An experienced agent will have a number of contractors, artisans, and interior designers on speed dial who can answer questions like "How much will it cost to install new cabinets, counters, and appliances in the kitchen? Can this bathroom be enlarged? Can we add on a room?" They want the work and will be happy to come out and view a home you're serious about buying to help you in your decision. But remember, it's still your choice who you work with.

Cost versus Value

One of the major benefits of owning an existing home is customizing it to your preferences and needs, including moving walls, adding on space, and remodeling kitchens and baths. To understand more about the cost versus value of remodeling, see Chapter 9.

The point is, don't be afraid to buy an existing home just because it's older or smaller. As you recall from Chapter 5, existing homes are often cozy and compact, but there is always a market for smaller families or singles who don't want the upkeep of a lot of square footage. It's the same philosophy as a hybrid car—smaller homes with better features.

Don't Expect Perfection

Many homes you view will already be in showcase condition, because they will be marketed by agents who encourage and support sellers to put their best foot forward with their home. The homes will be clean, decluttered, freshly painted, and repaired. Chances are that a home on the market is a home ready for company, so consider yourself a welcome guest as you come through the front door.

As with any home, you're going to be either impressed or unimpressed with the drive-up appeal. Think like an investor: Is the drive-up something that can be inexpensively changed? Would landscaping or a new front door help the look of the home?

It's easy to respond to a home emotionally because homes can remind you of *home*. A built-in hutch in the breakfast room can remind you of your grandmother and how she used to love baking you cookies. This return to your childhood may give you a rush of delight. A home can also dazzle, making it easy for you to fall in love, but that home may be a bit out of your reach.

It's important to be aware of how you will enjoy the home, but try not to let emotions get the better of you. Think instead of daily practical living. When you do your laundry, where can you fold your clothes? How easy is it to get groceries from the car to the kitchen?

For your first walk-through, you want to get the feel of the house. This is not the time to open the cabinets and count the number of cans you can fit into the pantry. You want an overview. Some features may jump out at you, like a beautiful view of the backyard from the kitchen and den. Imagine yourself taking advantage of it with furniture that will allow you to use the room and still enjoy the views.

Take along your schedule so you can get an idea of how you would live in the house, from going to work every morning to sleeping late on the weekends. What activities do you see yourself doing, and can you do them well in this house? What do you need? What's missing?

Jot down the features you like and what you don't like, even if they are small, and you may find that the small things simply don't matter when it comes time to make your selection. If the only thing you don't like is the paint job, you'll have a pretty good time in your new home.

Be sure to make a note about the items that will cost the most to replace and when they might need replacement:

- Roof.
- Air and heat systems.
- Plumbing.
- Appliances.

- Water heater.

- Windows.

- Fixtures such as sinks or commodes.

- Sewer line condition (older homes could be on the verge of replacement, which is usually a cost to the homeowner up to the center sewer point).

Peter Miller, author of *The Common Sense Mortgage* (HarperCollins, 1987), says it best: Is there a way to increase an existing home's value and utility, and is it worth trying? He suggests that you have the following options:

- *Do nothing.* If smaller homes worked for families 50 years ago, why change? Such homes are, or can be, perfectly habitable—especially for small households.

- *Renovate.* With this option you can take the basic house and fix it up with new kitchens, baths, electrical work, and other improvements. This is a good choice for folks who like their current home and have no interest in moving or enlarging.

- *Expand.* In this case we take the basic house and add on. This needs to be done with care. For example, additional cubic footage will require a larger heating and air-conditioning system. Also, some expansions are impractical. A five-bedroom home with a tiny kitchen may not work on a daily basis.

- *Tear it down.* With a teardown you remove the current home and replace it with entirely new construction. The result is a big, buildable lot with mature trees, a close-in location and—in a short time—a modern and larger home.

Your agent can supply you with market information that will give you the comparable market analysis you need to decide what's best for you, your family, and your lifestyle. Typically, if a home needs too much work, it might be a candidate to tear down. If so, the price should reflect the home's condition. On the other hand, an updated, well-maintained home will fetch much closer to new home prices because of the care the owners have shown.

Buying an Historic Home

The advantages of owning an historic house often outweigh the work that goes into finding and securing the property. There is a rewarding sense of history in the unique detailing and meticulous craftsmanship found in historic homes, as well as the satisfaction of restoring the home to its former glory.

A home that qualifies as an historic property may be listed individually or as part of an historic district. The listing of a building or district in the National Park Service's "National Register of Historic Places" provides public recognition of its importance, but will not interfere with an owner's right to alter, sell, or determine how an individual property may be used. However, city-designated historical areas or homes may have strict rules for the restoration of the home.

The benefits can be great—from reductions in property taxes and adjustments to assessed value, to state income tax credits and property tax freezes for qualified rehabilitation and restorations.

The National Trust for Historic Preservation reports that most states and the District of Columbia have laws that provide individuals with incentives for owning historic properties that meet their criteria—and not all older homes do. For more information on historical properties in your area, contact the National Conference of State Historic Preservation Officers at www.ncshpo.org.

Things to Consider Before Purchasing an Historic Home

- What regulations govern local historic buildings and districts?

- What about lead paint, asbestos, or other environmental hazards? Will there be problems restoring the home?

- How much restoration does the house need?

- Are original or substitute materials available for repairs?

- Are craftsmen available who are knowledgeable about historical materials and building systems?

- How will the house be appraised?

- Have there been earlier alterations to the home that required permits? If so, were they properly obtained? In some locations, a new permit cannot be issued until former work is permitted and redone for inspection to today's code.

The Surprisingly Versatile Ranch-Style Home

Homes built from the 1950s to the 1970s constitute the largest inventory of resale homes available by age, according to the U.S. Census, so this is the home you are most likely to encounter.

In fact, between 1948 and 1968 about 75 percent of the homes built in the United States were ranch-style, low-slung, and horizontal-lined, either single-story or split-level. How attractive those homes are depends a lot on local culture. If they are considered architectural treasures, you'll find them in premium condition and selling for top dollar.

Ranch-style homes are being rediscovered by home buyers who are rebelling against long commutes and making the effort to re-populate the inner city. From young families to empty nesters, buyers are finding they like the idea of a sprawling one-story house with no stairs to climb.

The genesis of the ranch-style home, say housing historians, was the prairie home designed by Frank Lloyd Wright. Using low horizontal lines and open interior spaces, Wright revolutionized the American home at the turn of the twentieth century. Other influences include the Spanish eclectic, which features stucco exteriors and Mediterranean elements to distinguish the design from the western ranch home.

While California builder Cliff May is known as the father of ranch style, it is probably Joe Eichler who is most responsible for popularizing the ranch lifestyle and sending it across the country. Eichler was a merchant builder who was among the first to hire nationally known architects to design and build housing for the middle class in large numbers.

But it was the automobile that really kicked the design into gear; ranch-style homes were often built with attached garages, an innovation originally intended to lower building costs, but they made up for cheaper housing costs in convenience.

Parents find the ranch home is family-friendly. In fact, home design is currently very retro, with an emphasis on machines (flat-panel TVs, computers) and family gathering places like dens, just as it was in the 1950s. Look at the return to low-slung furniture, and suddenly those eight-foot ceilings that save so much on energy costs start to look downright modern and cozy.

Boomers and seniors are returning to the ranch-style home because there aren't any stairs. According to Del Webb, one of the pioneers of creating active adult living communities, elders prefer the convenience of one-story living, but the rambling ranch is also well suited to young families who want large play yards, gardens, or pools.

To maximize your appreciation of the ranch-style home, consider the following:

- Look under carpets for hardwoods that can be exposed and refinished.
- Replace older sliding glass doors with French doors, which allow in the same amount of light with a more elegant touch.

- Strip and refinish wood paneling, beamed ceilings, and crown molding in contrasting shades to wall colors.

- Move walls to suit your needs. Most ranches have no interior load-bearing walls, so walls can easily be moved or eliminated for better flow.

- Add on for more space. An L-shaped ranch lends itself well to additions. Replace small master baths with cedar closets and add on a master bath with walk-in closets and a sitting room with French doors to the yard.

- Use new ideas in home design to flatter the ranch-style home with lots of light and horizontal lines, like the furniture suggestion earlier. Take advantage of continuing space with extra light and flow for entertaining.

Kathy Adcock-Smith, a member of the America Society of Interior Designers (ASID), suggests, "Our lives are enriched by materials that bring light into formerly dark areas. I call it 'seeing beyond.'

"For instance, in my mid-century home, in a set of louvered doors that separated the laundry from the kitchen, I replaced the louvers with sandblasted acrylic panels. The laundry now shares light from the kitchen, and when we entertain, the light in the laundry room has a pretty effect, and we are aware of an area beyond the closed door. The idea that the space continues adds to how large a space is perceived."

The ranch-style home has come full circle to being the right choice for many households today.

The Universal Home

Universal design has become an increasingly popular term for interior design that eliminates barriers. It increases accessibility for anyone with mobility, sight, strength, or hearing problems—either current or anticipated.

Baby boomers are just now hitting their stride, with the first group turning age 60 in 2006. If they're true to form, they'll want luxury and convenience in their homes, and will only grudgingly accept the infirmities of age. That's why the interior design and home building industries are working overtime to figure out ways to offer the concept known as universal design to all home buyers—from the disabled to young families with small children to the youth-loving boomers.

Universal design offers seven principles for your consideration: equitable use; flexibility; intuitive simplicity; perceptible information; tolerance for error; low physical effort; and size and space for approach and use.

The trick is making universal design features attractive and desirable, as ASID designers suggested back in 2001:

- Non-absorbing and easily cleanable bathroom and kitchen surfaces.
- Light-colored wallcoverings to add brightness to rooms. (Contrast light switches and chair and foot moldings with wall colors so switches are more easily identifiable.)

- Upgraded kitchen appliances with ergonomic features.

- Sturdy, lightweight furniture with rounded corners for easier access.

- Larger bathrooms with bigger showers and tile floors.

- Hardwood floors or low-pile carpeting with commercial-grade padding to give wheelchairs or walkers maneuverability. (Hardwoods retain value more than any other floor covering.)

So, as you can see, there is a wide range of choices with existing homes. You have lots of opportunities to turn an existing house into your dream home.

CHAPTER 9

Making Your Choice

You've evaluated several neighborhoods for their proximity to your work, schools, cultural amenities, and more. Hopefully, you've chosen the best neighborhood you can afford. Good candidates are neighborhoods that are likely to become hot in the future due to their closeness to existing hot neighborhoods. Whatever you choose, the neighborhood where you buy should be one you like.

Understanding the CMA

One thing that the real estate market proves is that home prices don't stay the same for long. While you can't watch the price of homes go up and down with the speed of a stock market ticker tape, changes in the marketplace can happen quickly nonetheless.

That's why your agent should provide you with a tool that we discussed in Chapter 2 to help you make your choice—the comparable market analysis (CMA). The CMA is a report derived from data collected from the local multiple listing service (MLS). Your agent pays a membership fee in order to access this data; it is not for the general public but for members to share with their clients.

The value of a good CMA is that it can give you useful information about the neighborhood where you are looking and the particular home you want to buy. Your agent can help you sort through the information so you truly have the best idea of the history of this home and its proper market value based on prices for other relevant homes for sale and recently sold homes in the neighborhood.

You'll learn what amenities are usually included among similar homes—how many bedrooms, baths, and whether basements or finished attics are usual. You'll learn how homes are valued by square footage and which homes have been updated, so you'll know why some homes are more expensive than similar homes.

You'll learn how desirable the homes you are considering are through "days-on-market" calculations that tell you when the home was listed. Your agent should also be able to find out if the home was listed previously and didn't sell for some reason.

You'll learn what the homeowner currently is paying in taxes, which can tell you a lot about when it was purchased and what it was valued for. Your agent can investigate further to find out exactly when the homeowner purchased the home and what improvements have been made, so you'll have an idea of how much the seller is making on the sale.

Your agent can also compute the list-to-sales price to help you understand what would be a reasonable offer. These are some of the many advantages of hiring a neighborhood specialist to help you buy a home.

A CMA is only as good as the most recent data, and its analytical value can change dramatically with the sale of any home in the report area. That's why it should only be viewed as a tool for right here and now, as the numbers can change by the afternoon or next morning.

Your CMA should include information on homes for sale and homes that have recently sold, but again, the length of time may be a subjective factor depending on market factors. (See the later sections in this chapter on buyer's and seller's markets.)

Online Market Valuations

Many lead generation sites that you may encounter offer free market valuation reports. While these are somewhat useful in a broad way, the reports are derived from tax roll data alone or sometimes limited data from other sources. For your purposes, these reports aren't reliable as the information is too general and possibly not current. In addition you could be missing key data, such as the reason a home might sell for quite a bit more or less than another similar home. That could be because of a number of reasons—the number of updates that have been done or where the home is located. (Does it back up to the highway while the home across the street doesn't?)

Your agent can give you much more specific information. She may have personal experience with the homes covered in the report. She may have shown the home to another buyer, previewed the home on an MLS tour, or sold the home previously. She likely previewed the home in anticipation of showing it to you so she would know first-hand whether the home should be included in your considerations.

A CMA typically includes the following data:

- Address.
- Original listing price to sales price.
- Lot size, structure size (number of square feet).
- Property tax information.
- Detailed property features (age of the home, number of bedrooms and baths, pool or no pool, garage, other structures).
- Notes from the listing agent.
- Photo.

Understanding Housing Markets

Housing is subject to the law of supply and demand, like any other market. Local factors such as the number of jobs available, the number of households moving in or out of the area, and the amount of new construction impact the price of homes, but so do national and world factors such as the cost of fuel. Mortgage interest rates are influenced by inflation and the government's tightening or loosening of short-term interest rates to cool an overheated economy or stimulate a sluggish one.

The Housing Boom

Like any home buyer or seller, you may be worried about the market following a housing boom. Booms always end, but that doesn't mean they end in busts. In fact, since NAR began keeping track back in 1968, housing prices have never gone down nationwide. Sales have slowed or peaked at times, or even receded, but overall, housing prices continue to beat inflation by one or two points, on average. If average inflation is 3.5 percent annually, housing values go up approximately 4.5 percent annually, too. But home values have been going up much faster than inflation in recent years. The median price of existing housing has gone up an average of 5.5 percent since 1989.

Certain areas have benefited from booms, but these are due to a number of factors such as jobs, weather conditions (the warmer, the better), the appreciation of coastal and other waterfront areas, the number of baby boomers who are of the age and have the wherewithal to buy second or vacation homes, low interest rates, and other positive factors. Your area may be gaining or losing population and jobs, which are the strongest influences on housing prices. Knowing where the marketplace is, in the general sense, will help determine your strategy in preparing an offer to buy a house.

Buyer's and Seller's Markets

There is no hard and fast rule about what makes a healthy housing market, but it's reasonable to assume that a market where conditions are favorable for both buyers and sellers is a healthy market. Certainly, stimuli such as low interest rates and new housing have contributed to revving up most housing markets.

But most real estate professionals will tell you that a healthy market, or a balanced market, is closely related to the length of time it takes to sell a home. In a typical market it may take three months to sell a home, while in an overheated market it could take a month or less. A sluggish market may see the process taking six months to a year because of a decrease in buyers. The amount of inventory (supply) also affects the length of time a home stays on the market. The greater the number of sellers, with fewer buyers, the longer a home stays on the market.

An unhealthy market is one in the extremes—an extreme buyer's or seller's market.

Buyer's Markets

A buyer's market is said to exist when there are more sellers of homes than buyers for those homes. The loss of jobs in a local economy can have a huge impact on housing. Also, the popularity of another area can cause households to relocate, which has happened recently to the "Rust Belt" states of Michigan, Ohio, and Pennsylvania. Some areas of the northeast have lost population to the Sun Belt states of the South—Florida, the Carolinas, and Texas. California is losing population to Nevada and Arizona, due to its high housing prices. Those buyers have caused housing to boom in Las Vegas, Phoenix, and other southwest metro areas.

Is a buyer's market a bad time to buy? If you think that jobs will come back and that your city has enough to offer to attract people to the area again, a buyer's market can be the best time to buy.

The advantage is on your side, because there are more homes for sale than buyers, so you have your pick of inventory, and a negotiating advantage with the seller. You can ask for more concessions and probably get them, including asking the seller to paint, to replace an older but not yet obsolete fixture or appliance, and to lower the asking price. Your agent will explain the market conditions to you and which negotiating tactics might work best with certain sellers, based on what she can find out by networking with other agents and analyzing the CMA.

Seller's Markets

When lots of buyers are chasing few homes for sale, that's a seller's market. In a typical seller's market, sellers can get more for their homes with little effort. They may even have buyers fighting over their home, with multiple offers, offers way over listing price, sight-unseen offers, and concessions by buyers such as no-contingency offers or "as-is" offers, as they are known in some areas.

Tips on Buying in a Tight Market

Increase your chances of getting your dream house, instead of losing it to another buyer, with these easy steps.

- *Get prequalified for a mortgage.* You'll be able to make a firm commitment to buy and make your offer more desirable to the seller.

- *Stay in close touch with your real estate sales associate to find out first about new listings that come on the market.* And be ready to go see a house as soon as it goes on the market.

- *Scout out new listings yourself.* Look at Internet sites, newspaper ads, and drive by the neighborhood frequently. Maybe you'll see a brand-new "for sale" sign before anyone else.

- *Be ready to make a decision.* Spend lots of time in advance deciding what you must have so you won't be unsure when you have the chance to make an offer.

- *Bid competitively.* You may not want to start out offering the absolute highest price you can afford, but don't try to go too low to get a deal. In a tight market, you'll lose out.

- *Keep contingencies to a minimum.* Restrictions such as needing to sell your home before you move or wanting to delay the closing until a certain date can make your offer unappealing. In a tight market, you'll probably be able to sell your house rapidly. Or talk to your lender about getting a bridge loan to cover both mortgages for a short period.

- *Don't get caught in a buying frenzy.* Just because there's competition doesn't mean you should just buy anything. And even though you want to make your offer attractive, don't neglect inspections that help ensure that your house is sound.

(Copyright 2006. Reprinted with permission from REALTOR® Magazine Online.)

Contingencies are requests that might include:

- Asking for a particular closing date that may be further away or shorter than the seller might expect. For example, you may want the seller to close after your kids are out of school.

- Asking for a feature to be conveyed that normally wouldn't stay with the house. What stays with the house can vary by region, so don't assume the curtains or chandelier convey with the house.

- Finalizing the offer upon inspection.

- Making the sale contingent on the sale of the buyer's home.

The better the buyer's position, the more contingencies he can request. Sellers may have contingencies, too, such as postponing moving until kids are out of school. In that case, the seller could rent back from the buyer until moving day. The cleaner a contract is, the more likely it is to close, but contingencies are a fact of life and should be expected.

Consider Remodeling Costs

While most agents aren't plumbers, electricians, or contractors, they should still be experienced enough to help buyers decide which home to buy based on the amount of work and costs of upgrading that the home will require. With that in mind, NAR partners with Hanley Wood LLC every year to do an extensive cost versus value report for *Remodeling* magazine. The report covers the costs, resale value, and percentage recouped at sale for 18 of the most popular remodeling projects.

The report includes some interesting data.

- A typical bathroom remodel costs $10,499 and can expect a return of $10,727 (102.2 percent return).

- A typical midrange kitchen remodel costs $43,862 and can expect a return of $39,920 (91 percent return).

- A typical master bedroom suite costs $137,891, but returns only $110,512 on resale (80 percent return).

The report is interesting because homeowners spent more than $139 billion on home improvements and repairs in 2005, according to data from Harvard's Joint Center for Housing Studies ("State of the Nation's Housing Report 2005"). As a home buyer, you should know what return to expect from a typical remodeling project.

Interestingly, the desirability of different remodeling projects varies greatly by region and metropolitan area. In the West, for example, window replacements are highly valued, perhaps due in part to insulation and cooling concerns in desert regions, with nearly 103 percent of costs recouped on sale. Westerners also prefer remodeled kitchens and basements; in this region, for example, a minor midrange kitchen remodel may return 112.3 percent, and a basement remodel is estimated to return 108 percent.

In the Midwest, however, the same kitchen and basement projects return only 85 and 73 percent, respectively. Midwest buyers appreciate homes with updated siding; midrange and upscale siding replacements return 96 and 98 percent of the project costs, respectively. Siding replacement projects fared well at resale in all four regions, likely because new siding is a relatively inexpensive way to update and refresh a home's curb appeal.

Buyers in the South are partial to upscale bathrooms, which return an average of 98.5 percent of project costs. When considering resale value, however, Southerners may want to think twice about midrange window replacements; this improvement, which is so popular in the West, only returns an average of 83.7 percent of project costs in the South.

In the East, a midrange attic bedroom addition returns an average of 98.1 percent at resale, but a home office remodel only returns 75 percent. In fact, remodeling projects that involved home offices were among the lowest returns on investment across all four regions.

In the final analysis, however, homeowners who are thinking about a remodeling project should consider their own needs and desires as well as those of the home's future inhabitants. "Keeping up with the Joneses can be a savvy investment move," says Stacey Moncrieff, editor, *REALTOR® Magazine*. "But ultimately, the best reason for a remodel is to enjoy it."

To view the complete report, visit REALTOR® Magazine Online (www.REALTOR.org/rmodaily.nsf) and click on the "Cost vs. Value Report" link under the "Special Features" section.

Buyer's Paralysis

You've seen dozens of homes on the Internet. You've also walked through at least 10 to 12. Now, you're ready to choose one—or are you? If you're feeling confused and can't make a decision, here's some help.

Home buying can be an overwhelming process. There are so many decisions to make, and any of them can mean serious financial consequences. A home, after all, is hardly a liquid asset. It's your greatest financial debt, even while it puts a roof over your head. As it appreciates, it also needs repairs and maintenance. With all that weighing on you, no wonder you've got commitment phobia.

Yet you really want to move forward. You know that few purchases will provide you the quality of life that a home of your own does.

It might be time to back up and examine what is causing the conflict between wanting to buy and being unable to make a decision. Here are some possible reasons you aren't able to move forward.

Fear of Spending Too Much

As you've learned already, lenders will loan you money at the top of your ability to borrow. Perhaps you think you might be happier in a bigger, better home, eliminating the need to trade up in a few years. This is a good strategy, but it may be putting more pressure on you. You must have confidence that your salary will rise, that your income is stable, and that you can handle large surprise expenses.

If you've been prequalified, you may already be looking at bigger, better, more beautiful homes at the top of your range. But something isn't quite right. Even though you may feel that your income is stable, a feeling is telling you that if you buy in this range, you won't have enough in reserves should something happen. Those are your instincts talking, and you should listen, because your desires have been doing the talking up to now. Your instincts are telling you to scale back your desires a little.

It's completely normal to feel this way. If you're really bothered, and not just gun-shy, remember that you can't go wrong buying slightly under your ability. Many financial advisers tell their clients to budget about 25 percent of their gross income for housing in order to position them to build reserves for savings, investments, home improvements, emergencies, and dozens of other reasons. That's almost 6 percent less than lenders will allow you to borrow (not including other debts). Just think what else you can do with 6 percent of your income. You'll still have your house, you'll just have more cash flow *to do other things with*.

A Conflict in Goals

Many couples purchase homes with the idea that they will have a child, so stretching their buying power to have the extra space to accommodate children makes sense. But if you are trying to accomplish two big financial goals at the same time—buying a home and adding to your family—sometimes something has to give.

You can't have it all—peace of mind, a large mortgage, and burgeoning expenses all at the same time—so prioritize your goals. In what order of importance do you want things to happen? What is most important to you? Whether you are planning a family, returning to graduate school, paying off a student loan, or buying a new car, you surely realize that your financial pie can only be sliced so many ways.

Your mortgage is the largest piece of the pie, and the larger it is the smaller the other pieces. Again the answer may be a less expensive house or a larger home in a less expensive neighborhood. If you are worried about cash flow, then making disproportionately large house payments will tarnish the joy of home ownership, unless you can find ways to cut down the other pie pieces.

Meanwhile, work to improve your cash flow. Accelerate paying off your credit cards. Don't incur new debt. Rebudget your expenses and eliminate unnecessary expenditures. Make compromises—vow to cut down if you can't cut something out. Be willing to move timelines for meeting your goals. Don't be influenced by others to live beyond your means. Set your sights on an affordable home, and you may find your dream home will appear right before your eyes.

How to Compare Properties for Ongoing Enjoyment and Value

Your agent has given you some great information that you can use to compare homes side by side. You've got your CMA and your home comparison worksheet. It's time to select a few homes to view. Refer back to your assessment of wants and needs to see which features are absolute requirements and which ones you'd like to have if possible. The following worksheet will help you compare the homes you view.

Home Comparison Worksheet

Comparing homes' features side-by-side will help you make the right choice.

Features	House #1	House #2	House #3
Address			
Price			
Location			
# Bedrooms			
# Baths			
Square Feet			
# of Garage Spaces			
Family Room			
Air-Conditioning			
Formal Dining Room			
Pool			
Spa/Tub			
Lot Size			
Landscaping			
Kitchen			
Floor Plan			
Storage Space			
Condition			
Curb Appeal			
Commute Time			
Other			

After evaluating the homes you've viewed, you may be ready to move forward by making an offer on the home you've decided is right for you. Depending on market conditions, you may have to act quickly. REALTORS® and probably your friends have stories about buyers who looked far and wide for their dream home, finally found it, delayed action, and lost the home.

The following are the most important considerations you have in choosing a home:

- *Price.* Most sellers will try to test the market to see how much they can get for their homes, particularly in escalating markets. You'll see some homes for sale without any comparables to support the asking price. Homes that are overpriced don't sell as quickly as homes that are fairly priced for the current market.
- *Location.* Some neighborhoods and streets have better reputations than others, allowing them to command higher prices for property. Locations that are hot are adding jobs, new community features, and new housing. Location is always worth paying for because others in the community are motivated to keep values up.
- *Condition.* Homes in premium condition will fetch the highest prices in any market, including a buyer's market.

The more move-in ready a home is, the more appeal it has. A home that has been well maintained and updated shows pride of ownership. Similarly, a home and/or neighborhood that has been allowed to run down raises some red flags, but also possible opportunity. If obvious maintenance has been overlooked, there could be some expensive repairs headed your way. Homes in poor condition invariably sell for less than similar homes in top shape.

But such a home can also be a good investment opportunity. If the numbers make sense, you can rehabilitate an existing home and help turn a neighborhood around. As more households move in and do the same, they are all part of revitalization, which is necessary to all communities.

Seller's Disclosure

In addition to your CMA and your home comparison sheet, you should also have a seller's disclosure that will help you in your evaluations.

Most state laws require that the seller come clean about problems they know about in the home they are trying to sell. Their disclosure is required to be in writing and address all items that can affect the value of a property. Since real estate is a state-regulated transaction, each state might require a different set of disclosures, but in most cases, disclosures will address the following items:

- The main systems—electrical, plumbing, gas, sprinklers, security, sewer.
- Appliances and fixtures.
- Structural problems such as foundations, water leakage, sloping floors, termite damage.
- Land and location—easements, noise pollution.
- Title problems.
- HOA rules and dues.
- Any damage to any item that could need replacement, such as pet stains on carpet.
- Additions or remodeling done that require permits.

What you can't count on is that the seller will be entirely truthful. Some sellers don't understand the importance of full disclosure; perhaps they're afraid that buyers might make a mountain out of molehill. And some buyers do.

The best protection you can have is to inspect the home with a qualified home inspector. (See Chapter 11).

Consider the Emotional Attachment

Don't let your choice of home be only about the numbers. Even though you were advised earlier not to let your emotions run away with you, you want *some* attachment there, or otherwise you might find your home fails to connect with buyers later on. You want to play up any individual, charming, and distinctive features your home has to marketing advantage. Chances are if you were charmed by that stained glass window, other buyers down the road will be, too, but only if it's showcased in a home that has been lovingly maintained.

The physical components and expectations of what makes a house a home can vary from culture to culture, but "the idea of home is fairly consistent, an emotional attachment to a place that offers safety and security," says Dr. David Kopec, environmental psychologist and contributor to *Realty Times*.

"For most people the notion of home is determined by how they perceive the place," says Kopec. "In many situations the home is simply an investment for financial gain or ensuring a child's academic success. Because we use our homes for so many different purposes, it behooves us and our agents to know as much as possible about how we view and conceptualize the home."

Kopec suggests that home buyers view homes in two ways: the physical components (Does the house work for daily activities?) and the emotional components (Do you feel good when you come home? Safe? Secure?).

Your feelings will be influenced strongly by whether your home is going to be temporary or permanent. If you're planning to move in a couple of years, you won't be as interested in making an emotional attachment, but keep in mind that "for children and adolescents, the family homestead is often viewed as permanent," says Kopec.

How satisfied you will be with your home depends strongly on three factors:

1. Personal characteristics (e.g., demographics, personality, values, expectations, comparisons, and aspirations).
2. Social influences relating to independence, security, privacy, and neighbors.
3. Physical factors, which include the psychological attributes of the physical residence.

Another factor that can affect satisfaction is how much you are compromising in choosing your home, or the difference between your preferences and your actual selection. This can be influenced by how much you have to spend, or how much you have to compromise with other household members, or how close you want to be to your work.

Being prepared with market realities will go a long way in helping you be satisfied with your choice and in your commitment to your home. In other words, you may have to learn to love what you get instead of getting exactly what you want.

CHAPTER 10

Making
Your Offer

If you are serious about the home you've selected, you must pull off a feat—accomplish two conflicting goals at once. You should get the best deal possible while simultaneously making your offer attractive enough to get the seller to accept your terms.

That's a balancing act that requires good intel, preparation, and negotiating skills. The intel comes from your agent in the form of the CMA, research on the past history of the home, and what she can learn about the seller's motivations. Preparation is your job—getting your finances in order and getting prequalified by your lender so you can make an offer with confidence. Last, negotiations begin with your motivation. How badly do you want this particular house? Negotiating with the seller's agent or the seller should be left to your agent.

One reason for this is that buying and selling a home are highly emotional events because there is money on the table. Buyers and sellers are inherently adversaries, but that doesn't mean the buying process has to be unpleasant, confrontational, or abusive to either party.

Sometimes that means paying the seller what he's asking; other times, you'll do just as well to try to buy the home at a lower price. What makes the most difference in your strategy is how far apart you and the seller are in price and terms and what the market conditions are.

Remember, the seller wants as much as he can get for his property, while you want to pay the least possible. That means that you both must try to reach a workable deal that will depend on compromise and give and take. Your agent should know which points are deal makers or breakers, and which will muddy the transaction.

If your agent encourages you to give in on a certain point, that doesn't mean she isn't representing you fully. Rather, it means she has your stated goal in mind: to secure this particular house. The agent on the seller's side is doing the same thing—trying to work a deal that will get the house sold, because that is what the seller wants.

Contingencies

Buyers and sellers have ideal prices, moving dates, costs, and other targets in mind. Sometimes you will have to make an offer that is contingent on another event, like selling your previous home, or waiting for the kids to get out of school. Or the seller may have a contingency such as building a new home and being uncertain of the closing date.

These are negotiable points, and sometimes a seller may be willing to take less for a home if their contingencies can be met, such as being able to rent back from you until their home is completed.

The most common contingency is a home inspection in which you pay a qualified home inspector to examine the structure of the house, roof, foundation, gutters, appliances, electrical and plumbing systems. The home should be conveyed to you in good working order, but that can change depending on your motivation. If you're planning to tear down a house or remodel extensively, you may not be as motivated to have an inspection, but if you are planning to occupy it immediately, a home inspection is recommended.

Understanding Buyer's Markets

As we mentioned in Chapter 9, there are buyer's markets at one end and seller's markets at the other, with balanced markets in between.

Each market varies with the amount of time homes take to sell, also known as days on market (DOM). Commercial brokers call this the *absorption rate*. When homes languish on the market for longer than what is considered normal (a subjective term calculated by how quickly other homes sell in a given period), the market is said to be moving into a buyer's market. Your agent will know the status of the market and its relevance to your offer.

Home sales are seasonal, with more inventory usually available in the spring, but a buyer's market can easily exist in the spring, if conditions dictate. Sometimes a buyer's market lasts for a long time. The exit of one or more major employers from a community, a natural disaster such as a flood or earthquake, or some other catastrophic event can affect home values in an area for years.

Whenever there is a surplus of homes, sellers will work harder to attract buyers by putting their homes in tip-top shape or offering incentives such as owner financing or a large redecorating allowance. As homes become more competitive, buyers realize that their interest is at a premium and they often increase their demands to sellers.

People who have occupied their homes for many years may be able to sell their homes at a profit in a buyer's market because they have built equity over time through rising home values and paying down their mortgages. But they may also find that if they have performed few or no improvements, the home will not sell for as much as other homes that have undergone improvements.

Homeowners who are most hurt by a buyer's market are those with little or no equity built into the home. If they are forced to sell, they may have to come to the closing table with cash to pay their mortgage off or allow the home to be repossessed by the lender.

The one certainty that can always be counted on is that one side of the market will never stay on top forever. In fact, it can turn on a dime. The same area that remains depressed for a period of time can make a comeback as lower prices stimulate buyers off the sidelines or investors who want to buy low in the hopes of selling high down the road.

Some Strategies for Buyer's Markets

- Be clear about what you want.
- The more homes there are for sale, the easier it is to get confused. Don't get derailed by the wrong house at the right price. If it's not going to meet the needs of your family or your investment goals, it's just plain wrong.
- Buy at the level you are comfortable.
- Buyer's markets may last a while. Just because a home is a bargain doesn't mean you should bite off more than you can chew financially. There should be plenty of homes that will offer you more than you thought you could afford without bankrupting you.
- Buy the best maintained or new properties.
- Because there are more homes on the market, sellers are competing for buyers, which means that they are more likely to put their homes in move-in condition. Unless you want a fixer-upper, let the seller do the work.
- Don't be afraid to ask for more.

Your agent will run through the numbers with you and show you what the lowest price you can offer is that will still be accepted by the seller. The seller's motivation, equity position, and goals will have a lot to do with whether they accept or reject your offer.

Understanding Seller's Markets

Seller's markets favor the seller because there are fewer homes for sale to meet buyer demand. Homes tend to sell quickly and for higher prices than they normally would, and with little bargaining between the buyer and seller.

Sometimes bidding wars happen, characterized by multiple offers from buyers. Concessions by the seller are less likely, and the burden shifts to the buyer to make the transaction as lucrative and trouble-free for the seller as possible.

One tactic that some sellers use in overheated markets is to refuse to entertain offers where the buyer insists on an inspection contingency, and they may even waive providing a seller's disclosure. This is risky for any buyer who feels pressured into taking a deal when it's much more prudent to know the condition of the home in advance of finalizing an offer. The seller may be using the condition of the market to avoid repairs that should have been made on the home.

A seller's market can blanket an entire city such as Las Vegas, a city that has the longest record for price escalation in decades. A seller's market can also be limited to a neighborhood, a city block, or even a single street. If the street offers continued desirability and rarely has homes for sale, it acquires a marquee value, like hairpin-curved Lombard Street on top of San Francisco.

A seller's market can be greatly stimulated by a robust economy and the higher salaries, job stability, and consumer confidence it engenders. The entrance of one or more major employers into a market is enough to kick off a seller's market. A positive national economic announcement may also stimulate home sales. Word of mouth also plays a part. A neighborhood that may have been in disrepair for a time may be revitalized by a group of buyers. Witness the urban renewal in many cities brought about by young nontraditional professionals, empty-nest couples, and singles, or the second and vacation home boom spurred by the Tax Relief Act of 1997.

Just because a home is in a seller's market doesn't mean it will automatically sell quickly and for a higher price. Value is still the great leveling factor in all markets. Even in a home buying frenzy, no one will buy a bad bargain. A home in poor condition or badly in need of updates will always discourage buyers because it will appear overpriced and too much work in comparison to move-in-ready homes.

Some Strategies for Seller's Markets

If you are planning to buy a home soon, and your area of choice is enjoying an economic boom, you'd better get ready for stiff competition from other buyers.

Seeing homes in which you are interested sell out from under you and at outrageous prices can be frustrating and discouraging. If you are in a seller's market and wish to buy a home, flip the odds back in your favor by doing the following:

Be Prepared to Buy Quickly, But Wisely.   Get your finances in order, clean up your credit, and talk to a mortgage broker or direct lender about becoming prequalified for a loan. Knowing how much you can spend can narrow your search and make it more fun. You will also be in a much better position to act quickly should the right house come your way. In fact, the more quickly you act, the less likely it is that the seller will look at other offers.

Pick an Area and Type of Home Where You Want to Live.   Decide on the lifestyle you want and what kind of home you want. Narrow your search criteria so your agent can network with other listing agents to find you a home before it comes on the market. If your agent isn't sure what you want, she'll have a much more difficult time describing your needs to other agents. Be as specific as possible. If your criteria need to expand a little in order to find a home, your agent will tell you.

Trust Your Agent to Find You the Best Home.   A seller's market isn't the time to look for a home without representation. If you don't have an agent already, find one who specializes in the neighborhood in which you want to live and the type of home you want to buy.

Be Willing to Sign an Exclusive Buyer's Agreement.   An agent who has a contract to represent you is a lot more likely to work effectively for you if you sign an exclusive agreement. Look at it this way—it's a commitment from you. If your agent finds out about a house that is coming on the market, will she call you or the other buyer who has signed a contract to work with her exclusively?

Don't Use Multiple Agents.   Unless you are looking at properties within a wide geographic range or in neighborhoods that require specialists to understand the demographics for those specific areas, one agent can fill your needs. Agents do more than research the MLS. They network with each other and in the neighborhoods where they specialize. If you want a home in a certain neighborhood, your agent will contact all the listing agents who work that area and tell them about you. Agents also work with local bankers to learn about homes in preforeclosure. They work with FSBO sellers to bring them buyers. The purpose is to get the jump on homes that need buyers but are not listed in the local MLS yet.

The worst thing you can do anytime you are buying a home is to attempt to beat the system by asking several agents in the same area to find you a home. Because agents network, they will quickly figure out they are working for the same buyer.

Tell Everyone You Know That You Are Looking for a Home. Get your own network of friends and family working for you, too. Put a note on the bulletin board at church, at the office, at the day care center. Drive through the neighborhood you want and leave fliers on the doors (don't use the mailbox—only stamped mail processed by the U.S. Postal Service is allowed). Tell these prospective sellers that you want to buy a home in their neighborhood and why. You'd be surprised how many sellers will respond to your enthusiasm. You may get lucky and come across a home before it hits the market.

Make Sure Your Agent Is Networking. It is against the rules of most multiple listing services for an agent to hoard a home once the seller has signed a listing agreement. The agent generally has 24 hours to get the listing into the MLS. But in a sellers' market, many homes change hands without ever making it into the MLS database because of the unique networking abilities of the agents. Make sure you select a strong networker whom other agents call when they have a new listing.

Make Your Offer the Most Attractive. If you have the opportunity to bid on a home with multiple offers, make sure yours is the most attractive offer. Make sure the seller knows how much you like the home, how prepared you are to buy it, and that you will make for an easy transaction. Keep contingencies to a minimum; the seller will assume that any contingency is a loophole to get out of the contract. In a seller's market, they have no reason to allow you to tie up the home. Make it clear that you are ready to move toward closing. If offers come down to personalities, a seller will want to convey the home to someone who appreciates it and poses the least amount of trouble, along with making the best offer.

Have a Tie-Breaker Ready. If bidding is close, make sure you can offer a tie-breaker. Offer to pay some of the seller's closing costs, and be willing to accommodate as many of the sellers' wishes as possible including move-out dates and closing dates.

Making Your Offer

As movie mogul Samuel Goldwyn once famously said, "An oral contract isn't worth the paper it's written on."

Your offer has to be drawn as carefully as possible. Your offer—or proposal, as it may be called in your area—specifies the price you want to pay as well as the terms and conditions you want both the seller and yourself to meet. Because real estate conveyances are state regulated, residential purchase agreements are standardized by state or local real estate associations to comply with the provisions required by statutes.

The following items may be included in your offer:

- Legal description (address) of the property.
- Sale price.
- Terms (cash, or subject to your obtaining a mortgage).
- Contingencies—conditions in which the contract isn't binding if they aren't met, such as lender approval, major problems uncovered by inspection, and so on.
- Length of time of the contingency period (the time required to get lender approval, perform inspections, and for the seller to provide disclosures, perform repairs).
- Seller's promise to provide clear title (ownership).
- Seller's warranties and provision to keep property in good repair until buyer takes possession.
- Closing date.

- Amount of earnest money to accompany the offer (a deposit determined by the price of the home and local custom, which is kept by the seller should the buyer default before closing).

- How the earnest money will be returned should the offer not be accepted or should the home fail to pass inspection, or should some other contingency spoil the purchase.

- Method by which real estate taxes, rent, utilities, are to be prorated between buyer and seller.

- Type of deed.

- Provisions for who will pay for title insurance, survey, termite inspections, and so on (also determined by local custom and/or market conditions).

- Provisions for who will pay for repairs or retrofits.

- State-required provisions such as contract subject to attorney review, disclosures.

- Provision for final walk-through inspection by buyer for closing.

- Offer expiration period.

- Legal rights and attorney's fee provisions in the event of breach of contract.

The purchase offer will become a binding agreement if it is accepted by the seller. If the seller wants to work the offer by changing some aspect, such as the price or closing date, the contract is not binding unless the buyer accepts the new terms. If the seller crosses through the original offer and writes in the change with his initials, then he is providing a counteroffer. If you agree to the counteroffer and meet the terms by initialing your agreement, you have a binding contract that will move forward to the next step—meeting other conditions of the contract such as home inspection and your lender's approval.

In some areas, contracts are handled by attorneys, but in most states, your agent will fill in a standard purchase contract form.

The Real Estate Buyer's Agent Council (REBAC), an affiliate of NAR, warns that while "most buyers and sellers are usually fully aware of the terms such as price, closing date, and financial terms, there is a tendency to overlook much of the preprinted portion of the form. Since all the terms of the contract are binding it is important to understand all of the terms that you are agreeing to before you sign the contract. Not doing so can be a costly mistake, especially if there are problems or difficulties in the transaction" (www.rebac.net).

It is highly recommended that you read and review the preprinted forms used most commonly in your area before you write and sign an offer to purchase. Your real estate agent can provide you copies of the forms and should be willing to explain and review them with you. Once a bona fide offer has been accepted, your focus will be on issues such as price, terms, and closing date.

By reviewing and understanding the purchase contract form ahead of time you can strengthen your negotiating position, protect yourself from incurring unnecessary costs or problems, and have a better understanding of what you will need to do to conclude the sale.

What Can Go Wrong

When the contract is accepted by both parties and becomes binding, then performance is required. In other words, you perform what you are supposed to do to meet the terms of the contract, or it goes into default.

Make no mistake, sellers and buyers have been known to sue each other for specific performance (a legal concept in which a court forces the parties to complete the transaction), so if you change your mind, find a better deal, or think you can make the seller sweat, you've missed your chance. If the suit is for specific performance, earnest money is not forfeited; the reluctant party is forced to go through with the transaction.

If you are already preapproved for a loan, go back to your lender and make sure that this home meets the lender's requirements for lending. If you aren't preapproved, you are working at a disadvantage because you have to find a lender and get preapproved on a deadline. If you are in this position, review Chapter 4, and start immediately getting the documents in order that your lender will require—W-2s, bank statements, investments, debts, tax returns for the past two years, and anything else the lender may want to do a quick analysis.

If you are self-employed, you must show tax returns as proof of income. Be sure to tell your lender your employment status before she gets started reviewing loan offers for you.

Lack of understanding about the loan process can get you into trouble. Make sure you don't make major purchases such as furniture, automobiles, or electronics anytime after contracting to buy your home. These actions could change your credit scores and cause your approval to be revoked or lowered to an amount that won't cover a loan to get the home you want.

Also, changing horses in midstream is a bad idea. While a preapproval is not an obligation to a lender, now's not the time to go shopping for lower interest rates. You should have done that when you got preapproved by comparing lenders. A last-minute change in lenders could cost you money or the house, especially if the lender can't get your loan closed in time.

Will You Save Money by Buying a FSBO?

Just like sellers who are represented by agents, sellers who want to sell their own homes want to make the most money they can. Often they will price their homes according to local market conditions, but almost invariably they price a little bit above the market, hoping to attract better buyers.

The number one reason FSBO sellers—or unrepresented sellers, as NAR prefers to call them—give for not hiring an agent is to save the commission, but few take the commission off the selling price of the home.

Buyers come along and see that the home is for sale, but they immediately encounter problems. If the owner is away at work, the buyer can't see the home until the seller is available to show it. Sellers may also be defensive about the price of their home, because they want the savings. In addition, they may have trouble understanding the paperwork, disclosures, and timing required of a binding contract.

Unrepresented sellers don't realize that when they put their own homes on the market, they are advertising to bargain hunters. The buyers know there isn't an agent involved and they want the amount of commission taken off the asking price of the home.

The bottom line is that both parties can't save the same commission.

The NAR began tracking the FSBO market in 1981; the record was 20 percent in 1987 following the oil embargo and the beginning of the savings and loan crisis. The number of unrepresented sellers has trended downward since peaking again in 1997 at 18 percent of all existing home transactions. In 2005, only 13 percent of sellers conducted transactions without the assistance of a real estate professional, and 39 percent of those FSBO transactions were "closely held" between parties who knew each other in advance, up from 32 percent in 2004.

One of the reasons there are fewer FSBOs is that the numbers work against them. The median home price for sellers who use an agent is 16 percent higher than a home sold directly by an owner, $230,000 versus $198,200.

Most unrepresented sellers are willing to pay a commission to someone bringing them a buyer. Your agent can represent you and still save you money if you want a for-sale-by-owner home.

CHAPTER 11

Home Inspections, Appraisals, Title Policies, and Homeowner's Insurance

In a few states, it's customary to have a home inspection before you make an offer on a property, but in most states, you'll have an *option period* after you sign the purchase contract. The option period gives you time to hire an inspector, have the inspection, and decide whether you want to live with the findings, repair items yourself, or ask the seller to repair some items.

No home is perfect, even newly constructed homes, and that's why you have the opportunity to examine what you're buying before you go deeper into the obligations of the contract. What you want to know about are defects of the home. The best way to do this is with a professional home inspection.

According to the American Society of Home Inspectors (www.ashi.org), a home inspection is an "objective visual examination of the physical structure and systems of a home, from roof to foundation." Like a physical exam from your doctor, the home inspector examines what's visible, and if he finds anything worthy of discussion, he'll make an evaluation and recommend remedies.

The purpose of a home inspection is to give you as much information about the condition of the property as possible. Your home inspection should cover the structural elements of the home, including:

- Foundation.
- Roof.
- Exterior surfaces (brick, wood, metal siding, stucco, concrete form).
- Doors and windows.
- Electrical.
- Plumbing.
- Insulation.
- Appliances.
- Heat/air-conditioning.

Outdoor elements should also be inspected:

- Driveways, sidewalks.
- Other buildings to be conveyed with the property, like garages.

- Porches, patios, balconies.
- Septic tanks.

Some inspection reports are more detailed than others, but that doesn't necessarily mean every item on it needs to be addressed by the seller. The inspection is merely a tool for you to use that

Hidden Home Defects to Watch For

No home is flawless, but certain physical problems can be expensive. Watch for:

- *Water leaks.* Look for stains on ceilings and near the baseboards, especially in basements or attics.
- *Shifting foundations.* Look for large cracks along the home's foundation.
- *Drainage.* Look for standing water, either around the foundation of the home or in the yard.
- *Termites.* Look for weakened or grooved wood, especially near ground level.
- *Worn roofs.* Look for broken or missing copings and buckled shingles as well as water spots on ceilings.
- *Inadequate wiring.* Look for antiquated fuse boxes, extension cords (indicating insufficient outlets), and outlets without a place to plug in the grounding prong.
- *Plumbing problems.* Very low water pressure, banging in pipes.

(Copyright 2006. Reprinted with permission from REALTOR® Magazine Online.)

tells you the immediate and potential maintenance and repair issues of the home.

Not every defect will be visible to the home inspector, so he has to rely on experience to tell him if certain features of the home might cause you problems. Certain appliances may appear in good working order, but may also have a short lifespan.

Inspections are often used as negotiating tools with sellers, but the seller doesn't have to address every item marked by the inspector. For example, a seller might have priced her home more favorably to you, knowing that it needed a little work, whereas a home in top condition would rarely if ever be discounted.

Most inspectors will be helpful to you in explaining which items are truly defects and which items are current or future maintenance items.

New Technologies in Your Home

Among the many considerations of home buyers is the use of electronics. If you're buying an existing home, you should check whether there are enough electrical outlets for the myriad of modern conveniences you own. New building codes require more electrical outlets than most existing homes have. If you don't have enough, you may have to call in an electrician.

How High Tech Is Your Home?

If the latest technology or entertainment options are important in your new home, add the following questions to your buyer's checklist.

- Are there enough jacks in every room for cable TV and high-speed Internet hookups?

- Are there enough telephone extensions or jacks?

- Is the home prewired for a home theater or multiroom audio and video?

- Does the home have a local area network for linking computers?

- Does the home already have wiring for DSL or other high-speed Internet connection?

- Does the home have multizoning heating and cooling controls with programmable thermostats?

- Does the home have multiroom lighting controls, window-covering controls, or other home automation features?

- Is the home wired with multipurpose in-wall wiring that allows for reconfigurations to update services as technology changes?

Visit the Consumer Electronics Association (www.ce.org/techhomerating) for a complete Tech Home™ Rating Checklist.

(Copyright 2006. Reprinted with permission from REALTOR® Magazine Online.)

Hiring a Home Inspector

Your real estate agent should have a list of home inspectors from which to choose. Another useful resource to check is the American Society of Home Inspectors (www.ashi.org). Like NAR members, ASHI members adhere to higher educational and customer service standards that go beyond licensing requirements. (Not all states require licensure.)

Ten Questions to Ask a Home Inspector

1. What are your qualifications? Are you a member of the American Association of Home Inspectors?

2. Do you have a current license? Inspectors are not required to be licensed in every state.

3. How many inspections of properties such as this do you do each year?

4. Do you have a list of past clients I can contact?

5. Do you carry professional errors and omission insurance? May I have a copy of the policy?

6. Do you provide any guarantees of your work?

7. What specifically will the inspection cover?

8. What type of report will I receive after the inspection?

9. How long will the inspection take and how long will it take to receive the report?

10. How much will the inspection cost?

Portions adapted from Real Estate Checklists and Systems and used with permission (www.realestatechecklists.com).

(Copyright 2006. Reprinted with permission from REALTOR® Magazine Online.)

Your inspector should be trained to communicate clearly, both verbally and in his written report. You're looking for someone with qualifications and experience.

You should ask what areas your inspector typically covers, negotiate costs up front (inspections are typically between $300 and $500, depending on the size of the property), and receive a copy of

What Your Home Inspection Should Cover

- *Siding:* Look for dents or buckling.

- *Foundations:* Look for cracks or water seepage.

- *Exterior brick:* Look for cracked bricks or mortar pulling away from bricks.

- *Insulation:* Look for condition, adequate rating for climate.

- *Doors and windows:* Look for loose or tight fits, condition of locks, condition of weather stripping.

- *Roof:* Look for age, condition of flashing, pooling water, buckled shingles, or loose gutters and downspouts.

- *Ceilings, walls, and moldings:* Look for loose pieces, drywall that is pulling away.

- *Porch/deck:* Loose railings or steps, rot.

- *Electrical:* Look for condition of fuse box/circuit breakers, number of outlets in each room.

- *Plumbing:* Look for poor water pressure, banging pipes, rust spots or corrosion that indicate leaks, insufficient insulation.

- *Water heater:* Look for age, size adequate for house, speed of recovery, energy rating.

- *Furnace/air conditioning:* Look for age and energy rating. Furnaces are rated by annual fuel utilization efficiency; the higher the rating, the lower your fuel costs. However, check other factors such as payback period and other operating costs, such as electricity to operate motors.

- *Garage:* Look for exterior in good repair; condition of floor—cracks, stains, and so on; condition of door mechanism.

What Your Home Inspection Should Cover (Continued)

- *Basement:* Look for water leakage, musty smell.

- *Attic:* Look for adequate ventilation, water leaks from roof.

- *Septic tanks* (if applicable): Adequate absorption field capacity for the percolation rate in your area and the size of your family.

- *Driveways/sidewalks:* Look for cracks, heaving pavement, crumbling near edges, stains.

(Copyright 2006. Reprinted with permission from REALTOR® Magazine Online.)

---

the inspection report as soon as possible after the inspection is complete.

Ask the inspector to e-mail or hand-deliver your report. A current trend is for inspectors to bring their laptop computers and input inspections while onsite. While more efficient, this practice may take more of your time than anticipated and doesn't always allow for the inspector to reflect on the inspection itself. Usually the buyer pays for the inspection and the inspector represents only them. If you want your agent or anyone else to have access to your report, your hired inspector will need to be informed.

Appraisals

Real estate values change constantly, resulting in the need to determine current value whenever a property changes ownership or is refinanced. Lenders hire appraisers (even though you pay for the appraisal) because they want to assess the risk of loaning you money to buy a certain home.

When you contact your lender to let her know that you have a contract on a property, the lender will review the basics of the contract in order to calculate whether you can afford the property, and to see if any of your financials have changed. If you haven't provided a full disclosure to your lender of your financial situation, now is the time to do so.

To help the lender in her decision to loan you money, she will dispatch an appraiser to your contracted property. The appraiser's job is to render an objective opinion of value, called a Uniform Residential Appraisal Report. Depending on his experience in the area, the appraiser will select comparable properties and look at the condition and features of your home. A lender's appraisal isn't used to determine market value; it is for the benefit of the lender to verify the property as security for the amount of the loan.

Lenders know that homes rise and fall in value, and because they can't see into the future any more than anyone else, they rely on current market value as the best criterion for determining risk.

Title Insurance

Local custom and the type of seller determine whether the buyer or seller pays for title insurance. In most markets, because the seller is conveying title, it is customary for the seller to choose the title company.

The title company typically acts as escrow agent (to hold on to your deposit and to distribute the lender's proceeds to the correct parties), facilitator for the paperwork of the transaction, and title policy writer.

A title policy is insurance you don't want to be without, but it can be costly—as much as 1 percent of the transaction. It insures against any devaluation or cloud to clear and free title that might occur because of incorrect information provided by the title company. The title company researches the chain of ownership to

---

Five Things to Understand about Title Insurance

1. It protects your ownership right to your home both from fraudulent claims against your ownership and from mistakes made in earlier sales, such as a mistake in the spelling of a person's name or an inaccurate description of the property.

2. It's a one-time cost usually based on the price of the property.

3. It's usually paid for by the sellers.

4. There are both lender title policies, which protect the lender, and owner title policies, which protect you. The lender will probably require a lender policy.

5. Discounts on premiums are sometimes available if the home has been bought within only a few years, since not as much work is required to check the title. Ask the title company if this discount is available.

(Copyright 2006. Reprinted with permission from REALTOR® Magazine Online.)

make certain that the seller has the right to sell and doesn't have someone else on the title of the home (such as a spouse) who isn't also on the sales contract.

You should know that even though you are paying for the title policy, it is required by the lender for the lender's protection. Some lenders will share a copy of the title policy with you, but to protect your own interests, you may need to purchase an additional policy with yourself as beneficiary.

Homeowner's Insurance

Lenders require you to have homeowner's insurance (often called hazard or fire insurance) on your new property that takes effect immediately upon closing. Because it isn't required right away, many buyers wait until the last minute to call up their insurer or go online to buy homeowner's insurance, but this is an important piece of the transaction that you shouldn't leave to chance.

Due to the high number of claims over the last few years, from mold to natural disasters like hurricanes, many insurers are limiting the number of new policies they write in a given area. In addition, the policies may be severely restricted, disallowing water damage claims that could lead to mold. In most locales, flood insurance is available only on a separate rider.

The sooner you start shopping for homeowner's insurance the better, as most lenders will not fund your loan without it, and many types of loans require homeowner's insurance to be escrowed, along with property taxes.

What Does Homeowner's Insurance Cover?

Homeowner's insurance covers what the policy says it covers, protecting you from financial losses due to storms, fire, theft, or other events. You must read the policy carefully so that there are no misunderstandings.

As many have found out, storm damage may not include flooding if the flood was found to come from another source. For example a hurricane may have blown the roof in, but flood waters may have ruined the first two floors of the dwelling. In that case, a homeowner's policy may not cover water damage, even though the events were related.

While you can purchase a policy that covers only the structure of your house and any outbuildings such as a detached garage or storage shed, you can also add other coverage:

- *Personal property*. This pays for household items such as furniture, clothing, jewelry, and appliances that could be damaged, stolen, or destroyed.
- *Liability*. This protects you against financial loss if you are found legally responsible for someone else's injury or property damage.
- *Medical payments*. This pays medical bills for anyone hurt while on your property.
- *Loss of use*. This pays living expenses if you have to move out of your home while it's being repaired.
- *Earthquake riders*. This pays for damages incurred from earthquakes.
- *Flood riders*. This pays for damages from floods.

Policies are approved by the state's Commissioner of Insurance. Some companies may sell more than one kind of policy. If you want more or less coverage, negotiate with your insurance company.

Why Does Homeowner's Insurance Cost More in Certain States?

Policy costs have a lot to do with the number and types of claims in certain states.

Insurers have access to a 10-year-old database called the Comprehensive Loss Underwriting Exchange Property Database (CLUE). This database tracks claims on properties and property owners. CLUE is a voluntary repository supplied by carriers of homeowner's insurance policies for the nation. It can tell an inquiring insurer the name and address of the policy holder, and whether there has been a claim for water, earthquake, tornado, fire, or other losses, and the damage claim amount paid. If the insurer thinks the house is a poor risk for another catastrophe, a homeowner's policy can be refused to the buyer, causing the buyer to look elsewhere for insurance.

Not only is the house subject to CLUE reports, but so is the policy holder. If you have had a number of claims, insurers might conclude that you are a poor risk, even if you've never been a homeowner.

The solution? Make claims to insurers wisely. Start shopping for insurance early. Notify the lender as soon as possible who your insurance agency is and what kind of policy you purchased to make sure you have enough coverage to protect the lender so the lender will make the loan.

Ten Ways to Lower Your Homeowner's Insurance Costs

1. *Raise your deductible.* If you can afford to pay more toward a loss that occurs, your premiums will be lower.

2. *Buy your homeowner and auto policies from the same company.* You'll usually qualify for a discount. But make sure that the savings really yield the lowest price.

3. *Make your home less susceptible to damage.* Keep roofs and drains in good repair. Retrofit your house to protect against natural disasters common to your area.

4. *Keep your home safer.* Install smoke detectors, burglar alarms, and dead-bolt locks. All of these will usually qualify for a discount.

5. *Be sure you insure your house for the correct amount.* Remember, you're covering replacement cost, not market value.

6. *Ask about other discounts.* For example, retirees who are home more than working people may qualify for a discount on theft insurance.

7. *Stay with the same insurer.* Especially in today's tight insurance market, your current vendor is more likely to give you a good price.

8. *See if you belong to any groups*—associations, alumni groups—that offer lower insurance rates.

9. *Review your policy limits and the value of your home and possessions annually.* Some items depreciate and may not need as much coverage.

10. *See if there's a government-backed insurance plan.* In some high-risk areas, such as the coasts, federal or state governments may back plans to lower rates. Ask your agent.

(Copyright 2006. Reprinted with permission from REALTOR® Magazine Online.)

Richard Collier, vice president of marketing and sales for Choice-Point (www.choicepoint.net), and the developer of CLUE reports, says that the CLUE reports are an important tool for buyers and sellers, but cautions that they can't be used to check out properties. CLUE property reports can be obtained by the buyer concerning his own claims records, but the buyer cannot access the seller's report except through an insurance agency, which may say whether the home is insurable, or the seller.

CLUE property reports are accessible online at www.choicetrust .com. Consumers can order one free CLUE report every 12 months.

CHAPTER 12

Homeowners Associations and Management Companies

With the explosion in popularity of multifamily housing, including condominiums, cooperatives, and planned communities, having *common* areas managed by homeowner representatives and professionals is good government. The homeowner side of the team is called the homeowners association (HOA), while the other part of the team is the property management firm.

HOA members are homeowners who generally get one vote per household. Board members are elected for a one- or two-year term, and the board or a committee appointed by the board oversees certain jobs like landscape maintenance, safety and security, and HOA bookkeeping. The board and its members also enforce the Declaration of Covenants, Conditions, and Restrictions

(CC&Rs) and bylaws, which govern resident behavior as well as use of common property.

Common areas are those land and building features that are used by all in the community, such as swimming pools, spa and workout rooms, clubrooms, lobbies, business centers, coffee bars, roads, fencing, parking, and more. In the case of high-rises and other condominium buildings, HOA fees might also cover building maintenance and staff.

HOA fees are assessed annually and paid either monthly, quarterly, or annually. The dues are calculated to cover normal operating costs as projected by the annual budget, plus reserves for long-term maintenance/replacement for roofs, pool equipment and tiling, paint, fencing, and other updates that add value to the property.

The board meets periodically to make decisions about expenditures, review the budget, and to address homeowner concerns. Depending on the size of the community and the board, the board may appoint special committees to address safety issues, architectural controls, landscaping color change-outs, and social events.

Condominium and planned community HOAs are backed by state laws to bind homeowners to their provisions, so they can't be ignored without penalty, usually a fine that is paid by the homeowner per violation.

Because you will need to know the HOA rules before you buy a home, you should ask your agent to get you a copy of the CC&Rs and bylaws, so you will know what is and is not permitted. For example, pets over 20 pounds may not be allowed in some buildings. If you own a 100-pound Great Dane, this may not be the home for you.

Homeowners can object to certain rules to the board—after all, the board is elected to represent the interests of the homeowners. The proper ways to do that are through a polite letter to the board and a member vote.

Sometimes a rule may change because the homeowners themselves have abused a privilege. An area that allowed pets or smoking might become off-limits because one owner didn't pick up after his pet or left cigarette butts lying around.

If an owner breaks a rule, it's uncomfortable for their neighbors to confront them, and that's one of the disadvantages of community life. If someone falls behind on their dues, or parks in the wrong space, it's the board's job to address it.

Management Companies

Because neighbors want to remain neighbors, many HOAs hire management companies who have experience in administration and property management. The management company may have its own property maintenance staff or may suggest companies to the HOA to hire for landscaping, window washing, and so on. These companies can assist with dues collections so neighbors don't have to confront neighbors if payments are late. They also have attorneys on staff who can review HOA documents in the event of a dispute or change.

Keep in mind, the HOA board and committees are volunteers, not professionals. They want harmony as much as the other members do, and are willing to volunteer their time for the greater good.

Many people choose multifamily housing to enjoy carefree living and access to more amenities than they might have on their own. For others, the sense of belonging—from the people to the ambiance of the community—is what draws them to multifamily lifestyles.

Insights into HOAs

A good insight into community associations is provided by a recent poll conducted by Zogby International for the Foundation for Community Association Research, a non-profit organization and subsidiary of Community Associations Institute (CAI). Their web site is www.caionline.org.

This telephone survey, which was based on interviews of 800 adults living in neighborhoods managed by community associations, found some interesting statistics:

- Nearly one in four HOA members had filed a complaint against another member.
- Nearly 90 percent felt their board was serving the best interests of the community.
- About 80 percent were positive they were getting their money's worth with HOA fees.
- Pets were the number one reason for conflict (28 percent).

- The best thing about a community association is carefree living (23 percent).

- The worst thing about a community association is restrictions on exteriors (15 percent).

What You Need to Know about HOAs Before You Buy

Community life is on its way to becoming the norm rather than the exception. Nearly 42 million Americans live in condos, co-ops, and communities governed by homeowners associations. More than 200,000 condominium, cooperative, and homeowners associations have been formed over the past 70 years, and about 50 percent of new homes in metropolitan areas are developed in a planned community format, says the Foundation for Community Association Research (www.cairf.org).

That's why you need to be able to protect yourself when you write your purchase contract.

"The initial offer should have an addendum making the contract contingent on receipt and satisfactory review of the last six months of board minutes," suggests Hank Sorenson, Florida real estate attorney and counsel for Prudential CRES Commercial Real Estate. "The purpose is that the board minutes would disclose all potential assessments and other minute details about the community that the seller might not know about or disclose."

Upon receiving the minutes, you should be able to go over them with your agent to see what kinds of issues might be under discussion for the property, particularly if it is an older property that has been converted from apartments. Find out if the HOA has a history of special assessments, which may suggest either poor planning, a conversion with a lot of trouble spots for owners, or a new community where the builder did not do a good job of making HOA covenants clear to understand. You should also get a copy of the HOA's budget for the current year to examine their financial solvency. It is possible that, due to mismanagement or unanticipated events, an HOA can go bankrupt, with association members on the hook for expenses they had believed were already covered. Solvency is paramount.

You can also get a sense of how the association is run and whether it is functional or dysfunctional. Do things get done or not? Are there large issues that aren't being addressed? Will you be annoyed by complaints that you see addressed in the minutes like noisy neighbors, barking dogs, and so on?

Of special importance is the *reserves*, that amount held aside for future expenditures such as renovation, roofs, and repairs. You need to know what expenditures have been made, which are planned, and which might require special assessments beyond your normal annual fees.

The home seller should also disclose to you what he knows about the HOA and its assessments. Has the homeowner paid a recent assessment? Is one owed? Sometimes at closing, you find out the hard way that the homeowner didn't pay a special assessment, expenses that are beyond the scope of annual HOA fees, because he figured he could leave you with the bill.

It is difficult to anticipate the needs of any community years down the road. For example, most HOAs have a landscaping budget, but that budget may not include cutting down, removing, and replacing diseased trees. Special assessments can also be instituted for major structural or construction problems like bad foundations. Homeowners may wish to add or remove an amenity like a swimming pool, which would also call for a special assessment.

To find more information on HOAs, visit the CAI web site at www.caionline.org, where you will find many useful tips about community life under HOA care.

Some Suggestions for Condo Investors

Sales of condominiums and townhomes have boomed for several reasons. Three of the largest home buying demographics are still in their youth: The baby boomers, GenXers, and GenYs, along with a strong immigration flow, are all helping to form more households.

Interest rates on home mortgages have hovered near 30-year lows for several years, allowing younger home buyers to enter the market. And tax incentives, such as mortgage interest rate deductions and no capital gains on homesteads occupied by the owner two years out of a five-year period, make home ownership attractive to everyone.

With homeowners able to sell after five years of buying their homes (as long as they have lived there for two of those five years) and keep capital gains under $500,000 for couples and $250,000 for singles, there's a terrific incentive to buy and sell homes in a serial fashion.

Can You Rent Your Unit?

Because the number of rentals in a community impacts home values, many HOA associations don't allow short-term rentals, and some try to limit the number of units that can be rented at any time.

Some builders are also discouraging speculative investment, by incorporating rules into the covenants that prevent buyers from selling their options on units, also known as assignable purchase contracts. Buyers must also take occupancy within a certain period and hold their units for a year after closing or until some percentage of the units are sold. In addition, homeowners who wish to lease their properties are limited to one- or two-year leases.

Selling Your Investment

Because investors must put more money down than homeowners and pay higher interest and capital gains taxes, many have figured out ways to beat the system. They buy with little money down, move into a low-maintenance condo for two years, rent the property, move out, and buy another property with little money down.

Some are willing to take monthly losses in rental income that is too low to offset holding costs, in the hopes that rapid appreciation will enable them to sell at a profit when the five-year period is up. Keep in mind that you may like the idea of a condo because most maintenance issues are deferred to the HOA, but those HOA fees may put the cost of carrying the condo higher than market rents will cover.

But each time you sell, you incur significant transaction costs. There are other ways to capitalize on your property. You can hold the property for longer, rent it, and when you want to sell, use a 1031 Exchange.

A 1031 Exchange, or *Starker Exchange*, is a "section of law in the Internal Revenue Code (section 1031) which states that if you exchange one investment property for another—and if you strictly follow the rules—there is no gain on the disposition of the property you previously owned," explains Benny Kass, *Realty Times* columnist. "Since terminology is important, the property you sell (exchange) is called the 'relinquished property' and the new property you acquire is called the 'replacement property.'"

Because of the complexity of ever-changing tax laws and requirements, suffice it to say that a 1031 Exchange has to meet certain criteria to allow you to defer taxes on capital gains. First and foremost, your personal residence is not considered investment property! Investments such as "fix-and-flips" do not qualify, and their developers are not eligible for 1031 exchanges, says Gary Gorman, CPA (www.expert1031.com). "Fix-and-flips investing is buying houses in need of repair at a price much lower than market value, fixing them up, and then renting or selling them for a profit. Typically, you have to hold each of these properties, the old property and the new property, for a year and a day to qualify for a 1031 exchange."

To find out more information on 1031 exchanges visit one of the following web sites:

NAR's Field Guide to 1031 Exchanges

www.realtor.org/libweb.nsf/pages/fg408

The 1031 Exchange Experts

www.expert1031.com

CHAPTER 13

The Final Walk-Through and Closing

After the option period is over, the contract is in force until closing. By now you have gotten your loan and appraisal, your homeowner's insurance, and your down payment together.

It's up to the seller whether to allow you to view the home again, to show your family, or measure for drapes. Depending on the custom in your market, you may have one last opportunity to look at the home before closing, usually the morning of closing or the day before. If this is not typical in your area, you may want to negotiate a walk-through as part of your sales contract. This is your chance to learn if the home is going to be conveyed to you in the condition you're expecting.

What Not to Overlook on a Final Walk-Through

Be sure that:

- Repairs you've requested have been made. Obtain copies of paid bills and any related warranties.

- All items that were included in the sale price—draperies, lighting fixtures—are still there.

- Screens and storm windows are in place or stored.

- All appliances are operating.

- Intercom, doorbell, and alarm are operational.

- Hot water heater is working.

- Heating, ventilation, and air conditioning (HVAC) are working.

- No plants or shrubs have been removed from the yard.

- Garage door opener and other remotes are available.

- Instruction books and warranties on appliances and fixtures are there.

- All personal items of the sellers and all debris have been removed.

(Copyright 2006. Reprinted with permission from REALTOR® Magazine Online.)

By now, you have addressed with the seller any issues you want resolved, such as repairs and any other final negotiations. The final walk-through is where you will see if the repairs have been made to your satisfaction. This is not the time to add new items to the list, unless you see something that has been damaged or is missing since you put a contract on the home. For example, the homeowner's pet might have destroyed a carpet that was pristine when you saw the home, or the seller might have taken down the dining room chandelier. Review your contract—if the chandelier isn't mentioned, it wasn't meant to be conveyed to you.

Make sure your agent and the seller's agent are in good communication. For example, the utilities should be tested during your final walk-through. How can you tell if the lights are working or the toilets flush if the utilities have been turned off?

Builder Walk-Throughs

Generally the construction supervisor will take you through a new house to show you that all the lights, appliances, plumbing, and other fixtures are working properly. He will turn every light on and off, as well as take you to the circuit breaker box and show you which rooms the switches operate. He will show you how to change the air filter in the system and how to cut off the water in the event of a leak or flood. Most builders will only allow parties to the contract to attend the walk-through.

New construction walk-throughs require more attention as you are reviewing the finished work on your new home. In addition to all of the items mentioned in the preceding list, buyers need to check the finishing work as closely as possible to ensure the house doesn't have major visible flaws in the siding, paint jobs, and drywall. Have cabinet doors and drawers been installed properly? Are doors hanging properly and do they open and close properly? Is the house clean and in move-in condition? Is the carpet and all of the tiling installed properly and is it clean? If you are buying a newly constructed home, make sure you take the time to review everything closely during your final walk-through to ensure that it's in good shape. Create a list of fixes and negotiate a time frame with the builder as to when they will be corrected.

By the time you finish, you should know where every light switch is, where your circuit breaker box is and any other system that requires maintenance. Your warranty books for your appliances and fixtures are usually left on the kitchen countertop.

Good builders usually schedule the walk-through several days before closing, so they have time to address any issues immediately. You should make a written punch list that the builder and you will both follow. This can include items with scratches or areas that need touchup painting. On closing day, you'll be invited back to see what has been completed. If your builder is unable to finish the work, make sure that funds are set aside in escrow to do so and that you agree on a firm and reasonable time period for completing the work. For example, your home may be ready, but due to a hurricane three states away, your builder didn't receive the fencing material he expected. In this case, it's reasonable to give the builder time to complete the fence after closing. Just make sure it's all in writing.

One thing that guarantees that your new home is ready to move into is a certificate of occupancy. This assures the city that the building has passed all city code inspections.

Be sure that you also have copies of all blueprints, floor plans, and surveys associated with your home. This is a benefit when it comes time to sell, as it only adds to the uniqueness of your home.

What to Do If There's a Problem

If there is a problem with the seller moving out, you'll generally know this beforehand, but sometimes your walk-through finds the seller still at home with nothing packed, or with items missing that you thought came with the house at closing.

If your real estate agent didn't accompany you to the final walk-through, immediately get in touch and relay the problem. Sometimes the problem is fixable immediately, or it can be negotiated at closing.

If you do find something wrong, this is not the time to delay the closing. Go ahead and attend, and make sure that funding to the seller only takes place when the problems have been addressed to your satisfaction. The seller's proceeds can be held in escrow by the closing agent until all parties are satisfied.

What to Expect at Closing

Along with your final walk-through, a few days before closing, you'll receive your final closing statement (also known as a HUD-1 statement), according to the customs of the area where you live. Your lender provides this in advance so you know how much money you will need to bring to the closing. Go over the calculations and make sure that the closing statement matches as closely as possible the good faith estimate you received from your lender.

Review the preliminary report of your title insurance, to make sure that the title company has your personal information and that of others who may be on the title correct. You and your real estate agent will also review that all the conditions of your purchase contract have been met, and that all directions to the closing agent have been given.

Depending on who is conducting the closing—in most cases, the title officer—you may be taken to a separate conference room from the seller. Sometimes the seller's portion of the closing is scheduled separately.

Most likely, you will be required to present your portion of the closing costs in the form of a cashier's check. The title company or closing agent will tell you how much you owe for:

- The down payment.
- Loan origination fees.
- Points (loan discount fees that you pay to receive a lower interest rate).
- Appraisal fee.
- Credit report (lenders often order one report when you apply for the loan and a second report to make sure you haven't incurred additional debt before the closing).
- Private mortgage insurance premium (this is a fee charged if your loan is larger than the typical 80 percent of the cost of the home).
- Homeowner's insurance escrow.
- Property tax escrow.
- Deed recording fees.
- Title insurance policy premiums.

- Survey fee.

- Inspection fees—if not already paid up front.

- Notary fees.

- Prorations of your share of costs for utilities and property taxes.

Prorations are costs paid on either a monthly, quarterly, or annual basis, such as homeowners association fees or utilities that may have been paid in advance by the seller. You must pay for your portion when you take over ownership of the home for the remainder of a given period. For example, assuming you buy your home on the sixth of the month, you would owe the gas company for the remainder of the month, while the seller owes for only the first five days. The bill would be prorated for the number of days in the month and then each person would be responsible for the days of his or her ownership.

Closings that used to be quite simple are now complex, thanks to a number of rules and regulations designed to protect consumers and other parties to the transaction.

What to Keep after Your Closing

The Real Estate Settlement Procedures Act (RESPA) requires that you receive the HUD-1 statement, which itemizes all the costs associated with closing. You'll need this statement for income tax purposes and for when you sell the home.

The Truth in Lending Statement summarizes the legal terms of your mortgage obligation and the agreed-on repayment terms.

You will receive a deed that transfers ownership of the property to you, along with affidavits swearing to the various statements by either party. For example, the sellers will often sign an affidavit stating that they have not incurred any liens on the property.

Riders are amendments to the sales contract that affect your rights. If you buy a condominium, for example, you may have a rider outlining the condominium association's rules and restrictions.

You should also keep copies of your insurance policies and proof of your coverage.

What Can Go Wrong

Most problems at closing can be prevented by good communication, particularly keeping the closing agent and seller informed of any changes that may impact the closing date.

According to a survey of 1,400 real estate agents in 2004 by Campbell Communications, about 12 percent of closings have to be rescheduled past the original closing date, and another 3 to 4 percent never make it to closing. The number one cause of the majority of these delays and lost deals, say about 73 percent of the agents surveyed, is "underwriting delays."

Other causes are also at fault for delaying closings, including "appraisal delays" (number two culprit) and "HUD-1s not available one day in advance of closing" (number four). The number three culprit is "Home buyer denied mortgage with initial lender." Thirty percent of agent respondents said "Seller unwilling to extend closing for mortgage delays" is also a significant reason why home purchase transactions fail to close.

One side effect of not getting preapproved by a reputable lender is that if the buyer isn't able to qualify for the loan, the buyer may be denied, or put into a different loan product that carries higher closing costs. Many buyers are surprised to find themselves at the closing table with higher fees to pay.

Another problem is not knowing the requirements your lender has to close a loan. Certain lenders, particularly those working with VA buyers and FHA buyers, have stricter requirements for the working elements of the property like the air conditioner and will use the inspection report and appraisal to issue a request to get a certain fixture or system repaired or replaced before the loan will fund. If the seller is unable to get the appropriate workpeople to complete the job, closing could be delayed. If so, you and the seller must stay in communication with the closing agent and your own agents.

One of the most common problems happens when the lender finds a glitch on your credit report that must be addressed. For you to arrange a payment or to find the appropriate paperwork and get it to the credit reporting agency in time is sometimes a challenge, particularly if the lender does a second credit check only a day or two before your closing date. As you learned earlier, these kinds of problems can be prevented by getting reports from all three credit reporting agencies before you apply for your loan and making remedies at that time. Also, inform your lender what steps you've taken and provide copies of all paperwork to and from the credit reporting agency.

Buyers can also delay closing by trying to get a better mortgage interest rate just before closing, but lenders need time to process the loan, and you may find that you pay more in fees than you would have had you stayed with the lender who already had your loan under way.

Sometimes the closing agent will be forced to delay closing because many people want the same time period to close, usually the last couple of working days in the month. This is to avoid laying out more cash for prorations. Avoid closing agent schedule problems by scheduling the closing at the first or middle of the month.

The closing agent may have a role in controlling the closing day. Check with the escrow officer to get an idea of how long it will take to issue the title reports and how long it will take to prepare the closing documents.

Another way you can save time before your closing date is to ask for a brief appointment when you can review the closing documents in advance so that the closing agent can explain what each provision and commitment means.

CHAPTER 14

Planning a Stress-Free Move

Moving ranks as one of the most stressful events in anyone's life. Not only is the planning and preparation time-consuming and labor-intensive, but moving also takes an emotional toll on family members and even on pets.

According to a 2004 study released by Royal LePage Relocation Services (RLRS), a division of one of Canada's largest real estate companies, women experience more stress than men with nearly half saying they felt irritable, anxious, or had tension headaches and trouble sleeping. Only about one-third of men had similar complaints.

Children react emotionally, too, as they are facing leaving friends and family behind and wondering if they'll fit into their new school and activities. Pets can't talk, but they show their distress by hiding, chewing, neediness, accidents, or other out-of-the-ordinary behaviors.

There are many strategies you can follow to make moving as pleasant as possible for your family, the most important of which is to get started early, particularly if you are moving at a high-volume time like summer.

You can manage stress by doing the following as soon as you know for certain you will be moving:

- Take a complete inventory of everything you own, with photos. This will be helpful to insure your belongings for the correct amount both for the move and for your homeowner's insurance, and to help in case you need to make a claim.

- Get together all documentation of antiques, paintings, jewelry, and other valuables.

- Gather and file all warranties, instruction booklets, and receipts for appliances and electronics you'll be moving.

- Gather all personal records, including past income tax filings, and keep them in a safe place for easy access. This should include all paperwork associated with your loan, purchase contract, and other documents associated with your rental unit, your current house, or your next home.

- Gather all sales materials, fliers, copies of contracts, credit reports, telephone numbers of workpeople, and everything associated with your move, into one place so you can access it quickly and easily. You won't be needing most of these items right away, and they will be safely stored in a safety deposit box until you're ready to get them again.

Moving Checklist

The following checklists will help you stay organized in the weeks leading up to your move.

Eight weeks before:

- Remove unnecessary items from your attic, basement, storage shed, and so on.
- Use things you can't move, such as frozen foods and cleaning supplies.
- Secure a floor plan of your new residence to help you decide what to keep.
- Start an inventory of your possessions. This is useful for insurance purposes as well as a review of what you have to move. Make sure to take pictures of things to document your ownership. If you have to file an insurance claim, these will be invaluable.
- Solicit estimates from at least three moving companies.
- Call your homeowner's insurance agent to find out to what degree your move is covered.
- Create a file for documenting all moving papers and receipts.
- Arrange to transfer your children's school records.

Six weeks before:

- Contact the IRS and/or your CPA for information about pertinent tax deductions.
- Evaluate your possessions inventory. Do you really need everything you have? Can you donate anything to charity?
- Notify your friends, relatives, professionals, creditors, subscriptions, and so on, about your move.

Moving Checklist (Continued)

- Begin the off-site storage process, if applicable.

- Locate high-quality health care professionals and hospitals in your new location.

- Complete change of address via postal service cards or an online service for the following:

  - Banks.

  - Charge cards.

  - Religious organizations.

  - Doctors, dentist.

  - Relatives and friends.

  - Income tax bureau, Social Security Administration, union.

  - Insurance broker, lawyer, CPA, stockbroker.

  - Magazines (for assistance with this task, go to www.oneswitch.com).

  - Postal service.

  - Schools.

- Clean your closets.

- Hold a moving/garage sale or donate items to charities.

- Choose a mover.

- Contact your mover to make arrangements and inquire about insurance coverage.

- If relocating due to a job, contact your employer to see what costs, if any, they will cover.

(Continued)

Moving Checklist (Continued)

Four weeks before:

- Send furniture, drapes, and carpets for repair/cleaning as needed.

- Gather auto licensing and registration documents; medical, dental, and school records; birth certificates; wills; deeds; stock and other financial documentation.

- Contact gas, electric, oil, water suppliers; telephone, cable TV, or satellite TV; and trash collection companies for service disconnection/connection at your old and new addresses. Also ask for final readings.

- Request refunds on unused homeowner's insurance, security deposit with landlord, and prepaid cable service.

- Notify your gardener, snow removal service, and pool service, if applicable.

- Contact insurance companies (auto, homeowner's, medical, and life) to arrange for coverage in your new home.

Three weeks before:

- Make your travel plans if you are making a long-distance move.

- Arrange to close current bank accounts and open accounts in new locale, if necessary.

- Notify your state's motor vehicle bureau of your new address.

- Arrange for child care on moving day.

Two weeks before:

- Arrange special transport for your pets and plants.

- Service your car for the trip if you are making a long-distance move.

- Contact your moving company and review arrangements for your move.

If you are moving into a gated community or a high-rise, find out what procedures you and your movers will need to follow, such as obtaining security clearances or using service elevators. Some movers charge extra for moves where there are stairs, split-level floor plans, or moves involving elevators.

Most moves occur within 50 miles of the home buyer's previous home. Many items you will want to move yourself in your own vehicle, including your personal records, jewelry, or collectibles.

Moving with Children

Only you know if certain family members are going to take a move well or not, and you can tailor your approach accordingly, but in most cases, the sooner you tell everyone the better.

Children need time to process big changes, not the least of which is the feeling of the loss of control over their lives. There are many ways you can help.

- Attitude is infectious. If you're happy about the move, your child will have a difficult time being unhappy for long.
- Use the Internet, books, and other media to educate your child about where you're going.
- A move is the same to a child whether it's one mile or a thousand miles away. Be sensitive to your child's sense of helplessness that he won't be able to walk next door to his best friend's house anymore.

- Focus on activities your child will want to continue or try, but don't expect enthusiasm quite yet. Perhaps your daughter is on a soccer team—show her that you are researching soccer options at your next home. Contact the schools and recreational parks in your new area to set up an appointment where your child can meet her new coach and teammates before the move.

- Emphasize how and when you'll stay in touch with old friends. Whether it's through e-mail, a cell phone free long distance plan, or personal visits, let your child know you are thinking of these things for him.

- Let your child have some control over her new environment. If she wants to paint her room purple and that's helping her look forward to the move, well . . . it's just paint, isn't it? You can live with it.

- Contact your child's new school and find out if there is a teacher's blog or chat room that the kids use, where your child can get acquainted online with her new teachers and classmates.

- Remember that change is harder for some children than for others. Be sensitive to mood swings. They're a normal expression of fear, frustration, and even anger.

- Help your child pack his belongings, starting with items he won't need at first, such as winter clothes. As he gets used to making decisions about what to keep and what to donate or throw away, he'll adjust to the idea of moving, and may begin to look forward to it. Needless to say, favorite items such as books or toys should stay with the child.

- Bank on things you'll do when you get to your new home. If having a home of your own means you'll have a dog for the first time, let your child search the Internet or books for information about breeds of dogs or training materials.

- It can take up to about 16 months for adults and children to adjust to a move. Don't expect them to be acclimated before you are!

Something fun you can do with your whole family is to make large, easy-to-read copies of your new floor plan (if you don't have one, you can draw one from memory to scale) and give each family member a copy so they can plan their furnishings for their new rooms.

Take measurements of your furnishings so you'll know in advance if that table fits where you plan it to go. As you decide what goes where, make notes on your master floor plan so you'll remember where things go on moving day.

You can also use the floor plans to discuss with your family what to keep and what to move. This will save you time later as you try to edit your belongings to your new home. In many cases you'll have more room, but if you are scaling down, some tough decisions have to be made.

The sooner you start donating or throwing unwanted items away, the less you will have to do as moving day approaches. Do a little each day, even if it's only to pack and mark one box and throw out one garbage bag of junk. You'll be surprised how quickly your efforts will add up.

To Have a Yard Sale or Not to Have a Yard Sale

In the middle of moving, conducting a yard sale may seem like more work and trouble than it's worth. People often pay pennies on the dollar for items you once paid full retail for, and at the end of the day, you may not come out much richer. In addition, you have to advertise the sale, put signs all around the yard, price and sticker each item, and so on. (You also may not want to advertise that you are planning on moving.) The day of the sale, people come knocking on your door before the sun is up, and you have to remain alert and vigilant all day to having strangers in your yard.

But for some people, yard sales are fun. Here are some suggestions on how to make a yard sale work for you:

- Ask neighbors to join in. They can help man the event, as well as pay for advertising.

- More stuff means more customers. Even with the competition from your neighbors' stuff, you'll have plenty of business.

- This is a great way to get rid of stuff you don't value anymore, or stuff that's hard to get rid of, like old computer monitors.

- Make sure you have a permit, if you need one, or all your profits may go to paying fines.

A better alternative for most people is to donate their unwanted goods. The advantage to this is that you'll be able to deduct the full value of the item, according to tax laws, as opposed to taking pennies on the dollar. Plus, things you are ready to discard are greatly appreciated by others.

Charitable organizations often have moving trucks that can pick up large items. However, you should check with the organization you want to donate to and make sure it can pick up your items. You may have to schedule this two to three months in advance to ensure pickup before you move. A third option is to sell the items on eBay or similar web sites, but that could cause you to have to stop other activities in order to ship items to buyers. Another alternative is to deliver the unwanted items to a local eBay store or consignment store to sell for you. That way you're thinking about them, handling them, and moving them only one time.

Remember, anything you don't give away, throw away, or donate, you're going to have to move. Moving companies estimate moves by the room and by the pound, so ask yourself frequently, is that item worth paying to move?

If you need window coverings for your new home, they may take weeks to order, so be sure to plan ahead and have them ordered and installed between closing and your moving date if at all possible.

You'll also want your utility hookups to take effect after closing so that workpeople will be able to use the electricity and water. Also, arrange for the type of Internet connection you want, as well as cable or satellite TV. You may find that your cable service doesn't extend to your new home, and you may have to make other arrangements to get TV service.

You should fill out a change of address form with the postal service. Also, inform your bank and creditors so that you aren't penalized if a bill fails to show up on time for you to pay.

Save a master floor plan for the movers so they will know exactly where to move your things. Movers don't have time to memorize complicated color codes, so it's easier to simply mark boxes clearly with the room and level where you want them to go. This helps them load their trucks more efficiently for multiple-storied homes. Furniture pieces can be tagged with directions so they will know at which wall to place the beds, the couch, and the breakfront.

Choosing a Moving Company

Referrals are a great place to find movers. If you know people who have moved recently, ask them if they were pleased with their mover. Your real estate agent deals with people moving all the time—she'll know who's good, too. But be open to getting referrals in other places. Storage facilities are a great place to get referrals because people use movers to move their things to storage. They know who does a good job.

Most major moving companies, even if they are local, have web sites where you can visit and compare information, so do your research. As mentioned earlier, it is wise to get at least three quotes from movers. All of this collective information will help you choose the moving company that best suits your needs and budget.

Moving dates and closing dates don't have to be on the same day. It may serve you better to close earlier than you plan to move so that you'll have time to paint, install new carpet, or make other updates before you move to your new home.

During peak periods especially, such as summer and weekends, movers need plenty of notice, so start looking for a mover as soon as you know for certain you are ready to move. They may also cost more during peak periods, or charge a higher hourly rate on weekends or holidays.

According to REBAC, NAR's buyer's agent affiliate, peak periods include:

- The beginning and the end of each month, since this is when most closings take place.
- All holidays, but especially those where school vacations coincide.
- Summer months, since the majority of families will try to orchestrate a move between the end of one school year and the beginning of the next.

Moving companies will give you an estimate either over the phone or in person, according to the number of rooms of furniture you have and the number of floors you are moving out of or into. Ask for a written estimate and whether the estimate is binding, which means it's good for your moving date. You should also know how many movers you are being charged for. Make sure the mover is bonded and insured; a worker could get hurt while loading boxes, or one of your items may get damaged.

If your move is out of the area, your estimate will be based on the distance of your move and the projected weight of your shipment, rather than an hourly rate. In that case, you need to be even more careful about the amount of items you want moved.

Make sure the mover inspects each room for furniture and loose objects that will be transported, as well as storage areas at the house such as the attic, garage, basement, and outbuildings. The mover will need to view everything that will be going to the new location in order to provide you with an accurate estimate.

Moving is labor-oriented, so there is a wide range of services that you can take advantage of, including:

- *Packing and unpacking.* Are you willing to do this yourself, or would you prefer to pay professionals to pack some or all of your loose materials?
- *Boxes.* Most movers will sell you new boxes, and the prices will vary per company. Ask about used boxes, since some movers will allow you to drive to their site and select previously used boxes that remain with the company after moves are completed. If you will need a lot of boxes, gathering used ones will represent significant cost savings.
- *Special handling.* If you have unique pieces (like a piano), heavy pieces (e.g., woodworking machinery), or very delicate pieces (e.g., antiques), you might need a special quote that identifies special handling of the object.
- *Special packaging.* The movers may recommend that certain pieces be packed in wooden crates. Check the cost versus the advantages of this decision.

■ *Insurance.* Most movers have some level of liability insurance that covers their moves. However, it is worth investigating additional insurance since it is not uncommon for objects to be damaged during the move.

(*Source:* REBAC Homebuyer's Toolkit. Copyright 2006.)

While price might be your major issue, you may also have to consider whether your move can fit into the mover's schedule. Your mover of choice may not be available when you want. You also have to consider whether you are comfortable hiring a particular company. This is where talking to past customers will help. Contact the Better Business Bureau or the State Attorney General to see if there have been any complaints against the company.

The person who is providing the estimate will usually be your contact at the moving company and during the move. Is she experienced, confident, a good communicator, and seemingly interested in satisfying your needs? In short, is she someone you feel you can work well with during a stressful time?

If so, you've found the right company.

Easy Packing Tips

Buy lots of commercial grade tape, black markers, and/or large labels, and plastic bags for liquid items such as detergents and shampoos. You can buy professional grade boxes, or pick up strong boxes at your local grocery, liquor, or electronics store. Ask other people you know who have just moved. See if you can take empty boxes from your workplace to use for packing.

The smaller the box, the heavier the items should be. The bigger the box, the lighter the contents should be. If possible, mark "heavy," "breakable," or other clues on the box, so they won't be improperly stored. Packed items should not exceed about 30 pounds. Be sure to cushion the bottoms and sides of the boxes with packing materials before putting breakables inside.

More tips:

- Thoroughly wrap all sides of breakables, with extra padding for spouts, lids, arms, and stands.
- Tape electrical cords to the underside of electronics. Do not tape furniture drawers closed, as tape can leave residue that causes damage.
- Do not pack combustibles, flammables, corrosive liquids including household cleaners, jewelry, and important papers or medicines.
- Do fill a box on moving day with essentials like toilet paper, paper plates, coffee maker and supplies, hand tools and extension cords, and cleaning supplies

Tax Tips

Some of the costs at closing can be taken as deductions on that year's income tax return. They include any prepaid mortgage interest and property taxes (consult your closing statement). Points paid at the time of closing represent additional mortgage interest and may be taken as a deduction.

Many of your other closing costs are simply added to your cost basis for the property, so that when you sell, they will reduce the amount of capital gain you may have. Under current law, you do not owe tax on capital gain up to $250,000—$500,000 for a married couple, both of whom satisfy the residency test—that is received as a result of the sale of a home in which you have resided for two of the previous five years. Make sure to keep all of your records, however, including those for permanent improvements, which will also be added to your cost basis. You never know when Congress will change the law in the future, and these records may save you considerable money in tax owed.

On each year's income tax, you may deduct all property taxes paid on any real estate you own. You are also entitled to claim as deductions all mortgage interest paid on a first and second home. Your deduction is limited to interest on any amount up to $1 million borrowed to buy or improve your property, and interest on an additional $100,000 in equity loans or second mortgages. If your borrowing exceeds that amount, consult an accountant and an estate planner.

Moving Expenses

Many of your moving expenses can be deducted from your income taxes if your move is related to a job transfer or new job at least 50 miles farther from your old home than the old job was. Members of the armed forces also qualify for deductions when they are transferred to new stations.

Deductions are for one-way trips, and include:

- Packing, crating, and transporting household goods and personal effects for your entire household.

- Mileage for use of your own car in moving goods, yourself, or members of your household (or alternatively, actual gas and oil expenses).

- Tolls and parking fees paid during the trip.

- Storing and insuring household goods and personal effects for up to 30 days.

- Disconnecting and connecting utilities.

- Shipping of cars and pets.

- Transportation and lodging (but not meals) for yourself and members of your household while traveling to the new home.

Settling In

While it's tempting to get everything squared away quickly, there's more to your new home than your belongings neatly in place. You want to feel at home as soon as possible, and that includes becoming part of your community.

Save some of the unpacking for a rainy day, and get outdoors for some fun and exploration. Make a game of it with your family. Let everyone go to the Internet, find your new city or town, and pick out something fun to see or do that the entire family can enjoy. Buy tickets to a sporting event. Visit the zoo. Tour galleries and furniture stores to pick out one great new piece for your new home. Find the nearest coffee shop or watering hole. Get on your bikes and ride around your new neighborhood. Find out where the local dog park is and let your dog make some new friends (and you, too). Sign up for an exercise class, dance lessons, or a golf clinic. Try something new that your new community is known for. If you've moved to a college town, sign up for a lecture series. If you've moved to the country, try horseback riding. Get a season subscription to the community theater.

Don't wait for your formal rooms to be perfect before you invite your new neighbors over. If you're in a high-rise or community with a clubroom, meet new people by taking your favorite card or board games to the common area. Take your dog for a walk around the neighborhood—dogs know how to get strangers talking and becoming friends!

Join the school PTA. Offer to assist on the next school fund-raiser and to help the coaches of your child's teams with drinks, snacks, paperwork, stats, or whatever the team needs.

Moving can indeed be stressful, but it can also be a wonderful opportunity for learning, growth, and doing what you love. Happy moving!

Conclusion

Owning a home can be an enjoyable and valuable experience, especially if you understand the home buying process. The NATIONAL ASSOCIATION OF REALTORS® encourages you to take part in one of the key components of the American dream—home ownership. As this guide shows, there are significant financial and emotional benefits of owning a home. So take the leap and join the millions of people who own property.

Home Buyer's Glossary

ABR® Accredited Buyer's Representative. A designation held solely by REALTORS® who have met the educational and practical requirements demonstrating skills and knowledge to represent home buyers. Awarded by the Real Estate Buyer's Agent Council (REBAC).

adjustable-rate mortgage (ARM) A mortgage with an interest rate that changes, based on a specific index, after a predetermined number of years.

agency Any relationship in which one party (agent) acts for or represents another under the authority of the latter.

amortization schedule A timetable showing the amount of each mortgage payment applied to interest and principal and the remaining balance after payment is made.

From REBAC's 2006 Homebuyer's Toolkit. Copyright 2006.

annual percentage rate (APR)   The cost of a mortgage stated as a yearly rate; includes such items as interest, mortgage, and loan origination fee (points).

appraisal   A qualified appraiser's written analysis of the estimated value of a property.

biweekly payment mortgage   A mortgage requiring payments every two weeks rather than the standard monthly payment. The benefit for the borrower is a substantial savings in interest over the life of the loan.

broker   A person who, for a commission or a fee, brings parties together and assists in negotiating contracts between them.

capital gains   The profit obtained from the sale of an asset, such as real estate.

certificate of title   A statement provided by a title company or attorney stating that the title to real estate is legally held by the current owner.

closing   A meeting at which a sale of a property is finalized.

closing costs   Expenses incidental to a sale of real estate, such as loan fees, title fees, appraisal fees, and so on.

collateral   An asset (such as a car or a home) that guarantees the repayment of a loan.

commission   The fee charged by a broker for providing services related to a real estate transaction, such as marketing the property (for the seller), finding a property (for the buyer), and negotiating a purchase contract.

cost basis   The original price paid for an asset such as real estate, including any commissions or fees, used to determine capital gains or losses at the time of sale.

deed   The legal document conveying title to a property.

earnest money   A deposit made by potential buyers to demonstrate their good faith interest in purchasing a property.

equity   The difference between the current market value of a property and the amount owed on the mortgage(s).

escrow   A deposit of value, money, or documents with a third party to be delivered upon the fulfillment of a condition. For example, the earnest money deposit is put into escrow, held by the broker, bank, or other party, until delivered to the seller when the transaction is closed.

Fair Credit Reporting Act   A consumer protection law that regulates the disclosure of consumer reports by consumer/credit reporting agencies and establishes procedures for correcting mistakes on one's credit record.

good faith estimate   An estimate of closing costs associated with the purchase of a home.

home inspection   A thorough examination that evaluates the structural and mechanical condition of a property.

home warranty   A guarantee for mechanical systems and appliances, but not the structure, against repairs not covered by homeowner's insurance; coverage is for a specific period of time.

lien   A legal claim against a property that must be paid before the property can be sold.

loan-to-value (LTV)   The ratio of the amount of a mortgage loan to the appraised value or sales price of the property mortgaged, whichever is lower.

lock-in   A lender's written guarantee of a specified interest rate if a mortgage is closed within a set period of time.

mortgage   A loan secured by real estate. A mortgage is used by a borrower to pledge real property to the lender as security for a loan.

mortgage insurance   A contract that insures the lender against loss caused by a borrower's default on a mortgage.

net worth   The combined value of all of a person's assets, including cash, minus all debts and liabilities.

PITI   Principal, interest, taxes, and insurance: four components of a monthly payment on mortgage loans.

PMI   Private mortgage insurance: coverage provided by a private mortgage insurance company to protect lenders against loss if a borrower defaults. Coverage is usually required for a loan with a loan-to-value (LTV) percentage in excess of 80 percent.

point   One percent of the amount of the mortgage. Lenders charge borrowers a percentage of the loan amount equal to the number of points to cover the lender's costs. Sometimes borrowers pay higher points in exchange for a lower interest rate.

prime rate   The interest rate that banks charge to their preferred customers.

principal   The amount borrowed or remaining unpaid on a mortgage loan.

real estate agent   A person licensed to negotiate and transact the sale or purchase of real estate on behalf of a property owner or buyer.

REALTOR®   The registered collective membership mark that identifies real estate professionals who are members of the NATIONAL ASSOCIATION OF REALTORS® and subscribe to its strict Code of Ethics.

REBAC The Real Estate Buyer's Agent Council, a wholly-owned subsidiary of the NATIONAL ASSOCIATION OF REALTORS® whose purpose is to educate and support real estate professionals and to promote superior buyer representation.

sales contract Also known as a purchase agreement, the legal document that details the price and terms of a property sale between a seller and a buyer.

settlement statement A document prepared by a broker, escrow company, or lender, detailing the complete breakdown of the costs and disbursements in a real estate transaction.

survey A drawing or map showing the precise legal boundaries of a property and the precise location of improvements, easements, rights of way, encroachments, and other physical features.

title search A check of public records to ensure that the seller is the legal owner of the property being sold and that there are no liens or other claims against the property.

Truth in Lending A federal law that requires lenders to fully disclose, in writing, the terms and conditions of a mortgage, including the annual percentage rate and other charges the borrower will incur.

underwriting The lender's process of evaluating a loan application to determine the risk of providing the applicant the requested funds.

walk-through A final inspection of a home before closing to verify that the condition of the property and contents are as contracted.

Index